What's a Disorganized Person to Do?

Also in this series

What's a Disorganized Person to Do?

Stacey Platt

ARTISAN

Published by Artisan
A Division of Workman Publishing Company, Inc.
225 Varick Street
New York, NY 10014-4381
www.artisanbooks.com

Library of Congress Cataloging-in-Publication Data
Platt, Stacey.
What's a disorganized person to do? / Stacey Platt.
p. cm.
Includes index.
ISBN 978-1-57965-372-9
1. House cleaning. 2. Storage in the home. 3. Orderliness. I. Title.
TX324.P572 2010
648'.5—dc22   2009013493

Illustrations by Matt Armendariz

Printed in China

10 9 8 7 6 5 4 3 2

I offer thanks to my yoga teacher, Sri K. Pattabhi Jois,
for demonstrating that clarity is the foundation for
a joyous and accomplished life.

Contents

Introduction

No matter how big or small the organizing task or the motivating force behind it, the time and effort it takes to put your things in order is well worth it. I have been a professional organizer for thirteen years, and time and again I hear: "I feel ten pounds lighter," and "This is better than therapy." Getting organized frees up space—both physically and psychically—and inevitably results in a feeling of lightness and clarity.

As one of my clients, who was running a business out of her home, told me, "You end up feeling a lot better than if you had gone to a spa." I helped her to weed out paper, create a system for what was essential, and find organizing solutions.

Another client, recovering from a serious illness, wanted help sorting through twenty years of accumulated clutter. The process of letting go transformed her home into a healing space and revealed endless possibilities for the new life she wanted to create.

In *What's a Disorganized Person to Do?*, I've compiled hundreds of tips, tricks, and ideas to help you achieve a greater sense of well-being through organization. Chapter one outlines general organizing principles and strategies that can be applied to any situation, while later chapters offer specific solutions for every nook of the house. Want to carve out more closet space without renovating? Or learn how to get a human on the phone when calling customer service? Perhaps you need a definitive guide to what to save for taxes or want ideas for organizing your kids' artwork? Want to learn how to streamline all those digital photos and files? This book has all these answers and more—plus removable stickers that let you tag things you'd like to try or need to be reminded about.

There are ideas in this book for every room in your home, from organizing your entryway to advice on how to use a scanner. In addition, look for these special features:

ONE-HOUR PROJECT: Step-by-step instructions on streamlining specific areas of the home, from the pantry to the bathroom vanity.

QUICK TIP: An idea, product, or service that will instantly reduce clutter in your life.

 DOUBLE DUTY: Space-saving solutions that multitask.

This book includes many recommendations for the latest organizing and technological tools. Since these are constantly changing and evolving, check with a tech-savvy friend for any new developments. The list will also be regularly updated on my Web site, www.staceyplatt.com, as will the latest in organizing ideas, products, and solutions.

But, remember, take a breath and don't get overwhelmed. Tackle just one project at a time, and let your successes motivate you to continue. The best organizing solutions often arise out of specific circumstances, needs, and constraints. So seek inspiration from these pages, but tailor and tweak this advice to accommodate your own space and the unique habits and quirks of your household.

Happy organizing!

What's a Disorganized Person to Do?

General Principles

Whether one is born with the tidy gene or not, being organized is a skill that anyone can learn. For some, it requires nothing more than acquiring a new set of habits. For others, it means devising systems to support the way you naturally think and operate. This chapter offers a handful of tools easily applicable to organizing anything.

1 Three habits of highly organized people

1. Consume consciously. To have a light, healthy body, we have to be conscious of what we eat. To have an efficient home, we have to make similar decisions about what we bring inside. Buy only what you love, will use, and have space to store. Let need drive your purchases. Do not be swayed by marketing promises, such as "bouncier hair," if you already have plenty of shampoo at home.

2. Spend your clutter. If only our money could multiply the way clutter does, seemingly without any effort on our part. Think of your home like a bank account: when you make a deposit (put something in), then you can spend some of it (take something out). So if you bring home a new T-shirt, you can give up one with holes, right? Just bought a fresh set of food storage containers? Collect the warped ones with missing lids and throw them away. And don't be frugal about spending your clutter. The goal is to get rid of clutter as fast as you acquire new things.

3. Live within your space means. Living within your *space* means is just as important as living within your financial means. Just as accumulating more credit card debt than you can pay off becomes a financial burden, accumulating more stuff than you can comfortably cohabitate with can be similarly burdensome. My five-hundred-square-foot New York City apartment forces me to simplify and let go: two endeavors that make life easier, less stressful, and truly more enjoyable.

2 Lessons from the silverware drawer

If I came to your house and asked you to show me your birth certificate, would you know where to find it? What about a safety pin? Your checkbook? The receipt for your computer? An extension cord? Your 2006 tax returns? Regardless of how many or how few of these you could produce without too much digging, I bet that if I were to ask you for a fork, you would know exactly where to go to get one. Why? Because the system for organizing your flatware demonstrates four organizing principles:

1. Forks are kept with forks.

2. They have a single and consistent home.

3. Everyone in the household is in agreement about it.

4. Forks are put back there after being used (and washed!).

These principles can—*and should*—be applied to organizing anything in your home. Keep like things together. Give everything a home. Get the whole household on board. Put things back when you are done. It's really that simple.

3   Think outside the container

The solution to conquering clutter is to *eliminate* clutter; don't just buy more containers, rent a storage unit, or move to a larger house. We will fill *any* container. It's human nature. But, of course, the more possessions we accumulate, the more items we now have to organize, clean, fix, move, store, protect, repair, find, rearrange, and worry about. In other words, the more stuff—especially unnecessary stuff—we have, the more our attention is taken up by trivial considerations. Thinking outside the container means stripping away what is unessential and identifying how you want to live your life. Then make your purchasing—and organizing—choices fulfill that vision.

4   Ten steps to organizing anything

The following ten steps can be applied to any organizing task, large or small:

1. Focus on the bigger picture. Why do you want to get organized and what do you stand to gain? In light of these goals, evaluate the quality and quantity of the things occupying your physical space. Once you've identified your big-picture intention for getting organized, write it down. Remember it. Begin to live inside it.

2. Visualize your desired result. Imagine your dream space. For inspiration tear out some inspirational pages from magazines, or whatever speaks to you. Having an image in mind, along with your big-picture intention, will help clarify what to keep and what to get rid of.

3. Choose an area of focus. Break down the job of getting organized into smaller, more manageable tasks, and focus on one small area at a time. Make each room a separate project, and subdivide further within each room. Start with a desk drawer, a bookshelf, a closet, the top of a dresser, etc.

4. Clear the space. Nothing says *possibility* like a blank canvas. Remove everything from the area you are organizing.

5. Sort into four piles. Use boxes or bags to sort everything into the following self-explanatory categories: Keep, Toss, Donate, and Fix.

6. Revisit the Keep pile. Ask yourself if you love and use what you are keeping and whether it reflects your big-picture intention.

7. Give everything a home. Decide where each item will live, keeping like things together.

8. Choose containers. Buy containers only after you know what you'll be storing and where. Measure the space where the container will go before you head to the store.

9. Maintain. Put things back in their designated place after you use them.

10. Tune and tweak as needed. As life changes, organizing also needs to change. Be willing to revamp your systems in order to keep up with your changing life.

5   The organizer's tool kit

Support your organizing efforts with the following tools:

1. Label maker. Choose a simple model for the ultimate tool
   in your organizing arsenal. Look for a comfortable keyboard,
   straightforward function, and portability. If you are used to a
   QWERTY keyboard, pick a label maker with one.

2. Bags and boxes. To stay organized while organizing, assign a
   bag or box for some or all of the following categories: keep, toss,
   donate, fix, relocate (to another place in the house), and recycle.

3. Measuring tape. Once you're done with sorting and paring
   down, measure the designated space before going out to purchase
   containers. You don't want to come home with a great product
   that doesn't fit the space.

4. Permanent marker and mailing labels. Stick a mailing label on a bag or box to clearly identify its contents and final destination.

5. Small notebook and pen. Jot down organizing ideas, products to buy, things you need to do, and anything else that comes up while organizing.

6. Tote. Contain all your organizing tools in a tool kit large enough to fit items 1, 3, 4, and 5 and handy enough to carry around the house. Try an actual toolbox, a plastic tote, or a basket.

6   Help with letting go

To help determine whether to keep a possession, ask yourself, Do I use it and do I love it? Use the table below as a guide.

DO I . . .	LOVE IT?	NOT LOVE IT?
USE IT?	Keep it! The things worth keeping are those that work perfectly with your life—or just make you happy.	Do you have a similar one that you love more? If so, let it go. If it has negative associations, replace it! Unflattering? Then out!
NOT USE IT?	Can you use it for something else? Can you pass it along to someone who would love it as much as you? Keep a sentimental item only if it has positive associations.	Are you keeping it because of a sense of obligation? Fear? Guilt? Then toss, recycle, or donate!

7 The physics of clutter

Clutter abides by the same physical laws as everything else in the universe. The second law of thermodynamics deals with entropy and states (in part) that:

- All things (including your desk) tend toward a state of randomness
- You cannot go from a disordered system to an ordered system without inputting energy

Unless systems are automated, they will require input from us. The tough news about organizing is that for your environment to change, there has to be *some* behavioral change. In other words, some filing is required.

The good news is that the time and effort made to get and stay organized is far more productive than the time and effort used trying to find an important document buried under a heap of other papers.

First Impressions
The Entry

The entry hall is the transition point between the outside world and your inner haven. The entry should create not only a good first impression on guests but also engender a positive feeling in anyone who uses it regularly. With a little organization, even the most cramped and chaotic entryway can be transformed so that it welcomes you home with open arms.

8 Five things every entryway should have

1. A landing strip, including a place for keys
2. A place to hang coats
3. Containers for scarves, hats, and gloves
4. Boot and shoe storage
5. A place to sit

9 What if I don't have a hall closet?

If you have the space, an entryway organizer or armoire can serve as a stand-alone closet. Otherwise, a storage bench with a cushioned seat offers a place to sit to put on or take off shoes, while baskets underneath store outerwear such as scarves, gloves, and hats. Hang coats and bags on a coatrack or wall hooks near the front door. Try staggering hooks at different heights to spread out the bulkiness of coats. Keep only frequently worn coats in the entryway, storing special occasion coats elsewhere. Mount a shelf above a row of hooks and put rectangular baskets on top to contain leashes and other dog-walking essentials, a lint brush, or small umbrellas.

10 The key to finding your keys

Always put keys in the same place. Get in the habit of dropping them in an appointed key catcher—a plate, bowl, basket, or hook in the area where you enter your house. If you have a hard time remembering to unload your keys in your key catcher, post a note on the outside of the door as a reminder until this new behavior becomes a habit.

How to organize spare keys

Apart from keys you use every day, such as those for the car, home, or office, there are probably many other keys—such as a neighbor's house or a second home—you need to keep track of. To easily identify keys, attach colored plastic tabs (available at any hardware store) that allow you to write on the label. Then assign a place for them, such as a framed piece of Homasote with labeled hooks or a more utilitarian version that can mount on a wall in the garage or in a utility closet.

11   What is a landing strip?

A landing strip is a designated place in your entryway, and *the* one-and-only place, where those important items you use every day—wallet, cell phone, keys, subway or bus pass—can land upon entering your home. It can be a table, shelf, or any flat surface. The purpose of the landing strip is to capture these important items so that you can easily locate them when you leave. A well-placed (and well-used) landing strip will ensure that these crucial items don't migrate elsewhere, which may result in a frantic search on the way out the door.

12   You've got mail!— so where to put it?

According to GreenDimes, an organization dedicated to stopping unwanted junk mail, the average person receives 1.5 personal letters each week, compared to 10.8 pieces of junk mail. The single most effective way to reduce mail pileup is to stop the junk from ever entering the house. That means taking a moment by the garbage can or to-shred pile to weed out insurance offers, sweepstakes offers, credit card offers, coupon mailers, unsolicited requests for charitable donations, and unwanted catalogs. (See entry 178, "Junk mail.") A tray on an entryway table can hold the rest of the day's mail until it gets processed. (See entry 167, "The daily mail," and entry 181, "Ten things you should shred.")

13 How to organize coats

• Instantly upgrade your coat closet, or any closet for that matter, by replacing mismatched hangers with matching ones. This will create a uniform look and give an overall neatened appearance to your coat closet. The best hangers for coats are wide-shoulder wooden hangers, which bear weight better than plastic ones. The contour of the hanger will keep the shape of coats, and the width will ensure space between coats and prevent them from wrinkling.

• To maximize closet space, hang short and longer coats in two separate groups. This way, you can utilize the space under the short coats to store other items. Face all coats in the same direction, noting that the curved side of the hanger (if it has one) goes to the front. If coat closet space is tight, then limit how many coats each family member keeps there. This will make it an active, user-friendly closet rather than a storage closet. Store off-season coats elsewhere. Aim to leave space in the closet (and a few empty hangers) for guest coats.

14   Presto: more entryway closet space

To create more room in your entry closet, look for dead or unused space. Is there a spot inside the closet where you can hang some hooks? Can you add a shelf at the top of the closet for storing items such as out-of-season clothing or a box of old tax returns? Is the back of the door being put to use? Try an over-the-door multihook coatrack to hold totes and handbags.

SHOE ORGANIZERS

A twenty-four-pocket overdoor shoe organizer isn't just for shoes. Use it for scarves, gloves, and hats in the entryway; wrapping paper and accessories in the utility closet (see entry 209, "Gift wrap and ribbon"), and action figures and Barbie dolls in kids' rooms (see entry 234, "Stuffed animal overload"). Small umbrellas can fit in the pockets as can baseball caps or pet accessories such as leashes and collars. See-through pockets make it easy to find what you need.

15   Here come the kids

Hi, Mom and Dad! Here are our: jackets, hats, scarves, backpacks, scooters, baseball mitts, and galoshes. Children are more likely to put their own things away if it's easy. For younger kids, hooks, pegs, and open-style cubbies are more user-friendly than hangers. If it's possible, assign each kid his or her own special place to hang a coat, leave shoes, and store a backpack. Individual cubbies work well for this purpose if space permits. If you don't have the room for those, hang a row of pegs for coats and backpacks at a kid-friendly level, about forty inches from the floor, and assign large canvas baskets, one for each child, to keep shoes contained and to prevent them from being scattered throughout the house. Keep only in-season shoes in the basket, relocating others to the bedroom closet.

16 How to contain winter wear

The best way to organize such winter accessories as gloves, mittens, hats, and scarves is to look for unused space in your entryway. Here are a few ideas:

· Drawers. If space permits, a dresser in the entryway or mudroom is a perfect place for winter accessories. Alternatively, stackable plastic drawers can be placed inside the closet under shorter coats. Drawers can be labeled, one for each family member.

· Sweater shelves. If you have about a foot of space to spare on your closet rod, hang a six-compartment mesh or canvas shelf and assign one or two compartments to each person for winter accessories, saving the lower compartments for kids.

· Baskets. Assign one per family member and store the baskets on the shelf above the rod in the closet for adults, or under a storage bench or on the floor for kids.

17 Take a seat

Entry hall chairs may seem old-fashioned, but they make a lot of sense. Whether you use an actual chair or a bench or even a stool, the idea is to have a place to sit when putting on and taking off footwear. Taking shoes off prevents dirt from being tracked through the house. Choose a piece of furniture that fits your decor.

18   How to stop tripping over footwear

If footwear clogs your entryway, two things are required: adequate storage and a limit on how many pairs of shoes each family member can store there. Try placing shoe cubbies in an entry closet or along a wall. Wet shoes and boots need a landing place. Rubber grids on top of a drip tray will elevate footwear to ensure that it won't sit in a puddle of dirty water.

19 Storing off-season clothing

- Always clean coats professionally before storing. Bugs are attracted to food and sweat stains. The best way to store a coat folded is to pad the sleeves and chest to maintain their shape and wrap the coat in acid-free tissue to protect against dust and prevent fading. If storing on a hanger, choose a solid wood hanger, pad the sleeves and chest with tissue paper, and use a fabric garment bag for protection against moisture and dust.
- Always store coats in a cool and dry place and preferably in a ventilated container or canvas bag so air can circulate and fabrics can breathe. Never store coats in dry cleaning plastic, as it holds in moisture and becomes a breeding ground for mold and mildew.
- The ideal space to store off-season clothing is in a cool, dry place such as an entry closet or a guest bedroom. Next best is to create storage in the basement, attic, or garage with something like a canvas clothes closet. Choose one with a clear vinyl window at the top (making it easy to see what's inside) and a bottom shelf for additional storage space for other off-season items such as sweaters and winter accessories. If hanging space is at a premium, plastic bins are another option.

QUICK TIP: **Winter versus Summer**

Use a label maker to tag (in a large font) one side of the storage box WINTER STORAGE and the other side of the box SUMMER STORAGE. At the change of seasons, position the box(es) back on the shelf accordingly.

20 Three ways to avoid mothballs and mildew

1. All-natural pest repellents. Mothballs not only leave clothes smelling like Grandma's attic but also emit toxic chemicals. Try cedar-scented products, which repel pests naturally. They are most effective when stored with clothing in an enclosed container. Adding aromatic lavender keeps stored clothing smelling fresh. Look for the one-two punch of cedar and lavender together in sachets or wood blocks and balls. Occasionally sanding wood products will refresh the scent and potency.

2. Absorb moisture. Add a chemical desiccant such as calcium chloride or silica gel to a storage bag or container to absorb moisture and prevent mildew. (Make sure the packets are intact so that the desiccant doesn't touch the garments.)

3. Use chalk. To reduce dampness in a closet and prevent mold and mildew, take about a dozen pieces of chalk, tie them together with some twine, and hang them from the ceiling. The chalk will absorb moisture in the air and neutralize humidity. Replace the chalk every three months.

Heart of the Home
The Kitchen

The twenty-first-century kitchen is the hub of the home: a place where homework gets done, art is created, plans are made, bills get paid, news is shared, and batter bowls are licked. Whether your kitchen activities consist of making elaborate meals or ordering takeout, the following organizational tips will make your kitchen a high-functioning—and pleasurable—place to be.

21 Take note of the triangle

In the 1950s, after hundreds of hours spent observing housewives at work, researchers at the University of Illinois determined that sink, stove, and refrigerator were best situated in a triangle, a configuration that smoothly connects these workstations to facilitate movement from one to another. For most kitchens, this layout is still the best arrangement. Keep the most frequently used items (flatware, dishes, pots and pans) within the triangle and store less frequently used items (such as stockpots and some appliances) outside the triangle.

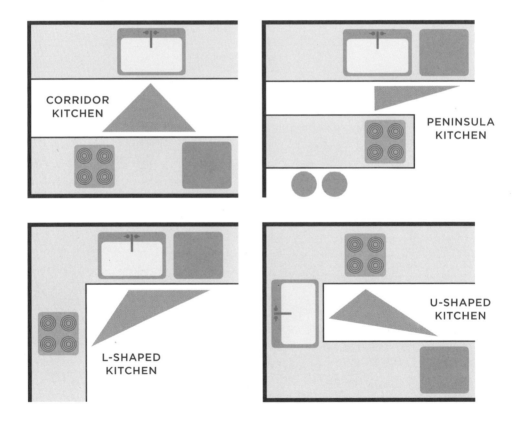

CORRIDOR KITCHEN

PENINSULA KITCHEN

L-SHAPED KITCHEN

U-SHAPED KITCHEN

22 How to reduce wasted effort in the kitchen

For some, this will seem like common sense; for others, a revolution: *Store things where you use them.* Keep pot holders, spices, and cooking utensils very close to the oven and near the pots and pans. Store dishes and silverware near the dishwasher, the colander and cleaning supplies near the sink. Cutting board, knives, measuring spoons, and mixing bowls go near the prep area.

23 Counter intelligence

The single most important component of an organized kitchen is clutter-free countertops. Countertop real estate is a hot commodity and should be reserved for items used frequently, if not daily. Relocate seldom-used appliances and gadgets to cabinets and drawers. Small items such as vitamins, supplements, and tea boxes have a tendency to accumulate and produce visual clutter. To get stuff off the counters, think up (to walls and ceiling), in (behind closed cabinet doors and drawers), and out (of the kitchen altogether).

24 Twelve ways to create more space in the kitchen

Look for unused space and find creative ways to use it.
Here are some ideas:

1. Look for unused wall space to hang shelves for additional storage.

2. Mount a stainless-steel bar with S hooks to hang a spice rack and/or utensils.

3. Mount a knife strip on the wall.

4. Even empty corners can be put to use; equip them wih slim cabinentry that takes advantage of vertical space.

5. Use wood boxes to store things you don't use regularly that might otherwise gather dust or be in the way.

6. Adjustable shelving can be customized to store taller items such as vases and jugs.

7. A butcher-block surface does double-duty as a top for an island and a cutting board. Add shelving underneath.

8. Use matching baskets to hold nonrefrigerated produce such as garlic, onions, and ginger.

9. Put the kitchen table to use. Free up drawer space by keeping flatware in a caddy in the center of the table.

10. Save counter space by mounting small appliances, like a microwave, coffeemaker, or toaster, under upper cabinets.

11. Buy two-in-one space-saving appliances such as microwave-toaster combinations.

12. Paint the walls. Lighter colors help make the space seem bigger and more open.

25 Tips for making the most of limited counter space

Food prep

- Buy small appliances such as toasters, microwaves, and can openers that can be mounted underneath cabinets.
- Swap a knife block for a magnetic strip on the wall.
- Instead of storing utensils in a canister, install a stainless steel rod with matching S hooks on the backsplash and hang utensils out of the way but still within arm's reach.

Cleanup

- Replace the bottle of dishwashing soap with a soap-dispensing dish wand.
- Substitute a dish drainer for an over-the-sink or wall-mounted variety.
- Replace a countertop water filter or pitcher with one that mounts on a faucet.

Storage

- Hang narrow shelves between counter and cabinets to hold everyday items such as salt, pepper, coffee fixings, teas, and vitamins.
- Relocate the fruit bowl from the counter to the center of the kitchen table.
- Hang a three-tiered wire basket from a plant hook that extends from the wall to contain nonrefrigerated produce such as potatoes, tomatoes, garlic, and onions.

26 Just say *no* to sink clutter

Keep all your sink accessories neat with a sink organizer that holds dish soap, scrubbers, and sponge in one contained unit. If you are short on counter space, ditch the scrubbers and outfit your sink with a stainless steel suction-cupped sponge holder to keep sponges off the counter. Sponges used for deeper cleaning are best stored under the sink. Swap homely plastic dish soap bottles for a stainless steel or glass soap dispenser. One trick is to use one liquid soap that multitasks as both a dish and hand soap. One variety is Biokleen, which not only cleans but is also so gentle on the skin it can double as a bubble bath or pet shampoo.

27 How to create a breakfast bar

Make morning rituals easy and efficient by keeping all your breakfast needs together in one area. Keep breakfast appliances such as the toaster, coffeemaker, or blender clustered together on the counter. If coffee is part of your morning regimen, contain the necessary accoutrements (coffee, grinder, milk frother, etc.) together in a box or basket near the coffeemaker. Keep sweeteners, nondairy creamers, and any other add-ins on a small tray to cart to and from the table in a single trip.

QUICK TIP: **Garbage Bags**

Take plastic garbage bags out of their box and put them in the bottom of the garbage pails they are meant to line. The next one is ready and waiting when you take the trash out. This not only frees up space under the sink but also makes bags handy when and where you need them.

28 How to store cleaning products

Separate the products used daily or weekly (such as dish soap, dish-washing liquid, and garbage bags) from products that are used occasionally (such as drain de-cloggers and specialty cleaners). If space is limited, relocate the less-used items to other parts of the house such as the utility closet, laundry area, or garage, according to their purpose. If you have small children, keep toxic chemical cleaners such as ammonia out of reach of curious hands. Store only often-used items in the cabinet under the sink and use the following, depending on your needs:

- Caddies. Make it easier to tote cleaning supplies.
- Expandable undersink shelves. Create more vertical storage by fitting around pipes.
- Sliding cabinet baskets. Get better access to the back of the cabinet.

29 One-Hour Project
Organize the jumble under the kitchen sink

1. Gather the following: a bucket, soap, rubber gloves, sponge, and garbage bag.

2. Take everything out of the cabinet under the sink.

3. Throw away bottles that are crusty, empty, old, or that you no longer use, keeping in mind that cleaners lose their potency over time, even chemical ones. (See entry 30, "When to toss: cleaning products.")

4. Dilute one part soap in two parts warm water to clean the cabinets. For stubborn stains and grime, mix baking soda and water to make a potent scrub. Avoid using steel wool or scrubbing brushes, which might damage the wood.

5. Take the measurements of the inside of the cabinet and line it with vinyl flooring (available at your local home improvement store) to protect the wood from spills and make it easy to clean. Vinyl flooring is inexpensive and easy to cut to size with household scissors.

6. Outfit the cabinet with the appropriate organizing products (see entry 28, "How to store cleaning products") and replace cleaning supplies accordingly.

30 When to toss: cleaning products

If a cleaning product is old, discard it. If there is clumping, hardening, or its color has changed, it's also time to throw it away. If the container is damaged, then get rid of it to prevent spills and leakage. And even if none of these signs are present, take note of the average shelf life of cleaning products to know when yours have lost their potency:

Product	Shelf Life
BLEACH	6–9 months
DISH SOAP	1–2 years
GLASS CLEANER	18 months–2 years
LAUNDRY DETERGENT (POWDER OR LIQUID)	6 months opened; 1–2 years unopened
WOOD POLISH	2 years
METAL POLISH	3 years

Crush empty plastic bottles and aluminum cans to take up less space when you recycle them. Rinse first and then carefully step on them to compress.

31   How to manage plastic bags

Most people squirrel away more plastic bags than they will ever use. A better approach than stuffing them under the sink is to choose a receptacle for the bags and never keep more than can fit in that container. Many stores now offer recycling drops for plastic bags—take advantage of these! Look for plastic bag holders that adhere to the inside of a cabinet door. A green alternative is to reduce your household consumption of plastic by bringing your own bags to the grocery store. Nylon or canvas reusable shopping bags that stuff into an integrated sack are light and compact and fit easily into a purse or pocket.

32   Recycle!

About 80 percent of what Americans throw away is recyclable, yet according to the Environmental Protection Agency, our recycling rate is only 32.5 percent. You can help make a difference by making recycling part of your daily routine. If you aren't clear about how and what to recycle, check local resources and guidelines by visiting the National Recycling Coalition at www.nrc-recycle.org/localresources.aspx or by visiting your city's Web site.

If no curbside recycling exists in your area, call 1-800-CLEANUP for the recycling center nearest you. Post the list of what can and should be recycled for easy reference. Set up bins for the collection of each type of recyclable material. Many new kitchens have recycling bins built into cabinets. You can also buy fully assembled sliding systems that mount easily to the bottom of a cabinet. Another option is stackable recycling bins, which can be kept in the kitchen, mudroom, pantry, or garage. Label bins for easy identification.

Then go one step further and purchase products that support the environment and reduce your recycling efforts. Avoid individually wrapped items whenever possible and choose products with the least amount of packaging. Check packaging and products for the highest percentage of postconsumer recycled content and use your purchasing power to support these earth-saving efforts.

QUICK TIP: **Where to Recycle**

The iPhone app iRecycle lists more than 100,000 locations for recycling or disposal of upwards of 200 materials.

the kitchen

33   Recycling resources

Type of Product	Recycling Contacts
APPLIANCES	Steel Recycling Institute (www.recycle-steel.org)
BUILDING MATERIALS	Habitat for Humanity (www.habitat.org)
CARPET	Carpet America Recovery Effort (www.carpetrecovery.org)
BATTERIES (HOUSEHOLD)	Environment, Health and Safety Online (www.ehso.com/ehshome/batteries.php)
CELL PHONES AND RECHARGEABLE BATTERIES	Rechargeable Battery Recycling Corporation (www.rbrc.org/start.php)
COMPUTERS AND TECHNOLOGY	Recycles.org (www.recycles.org)
COMPACT FLUORESCENT BULBS	Your local hardware store
EYEGLASSES	New Eyes for the Needy (www.neweyesfortheneedy.org)
FORMAL DRESSES	Operation Fairy Dust (www.operationfairydust.org)
MOTOR OIL (USED)	Your local service station
PAINT	Earth 911 (www.earth911.org) or a local waste facility
PRINTER INK CARTRIDGES	Your local office supply store
STYROFOAM PEANUTS	UPS stores (www.ups.com) or the Plastic Loose Fill Council (www.loosefillpackaging.com/search)
VEHICLES	Ask if your favorite nonprofit accepts car donations

34 A word on dish towels

Choose linen over cotton for drying dishes. Linen, an organic fiber woven from flax, is stronger, more absorbent, and lasts longer than cotton. A lint-free fiber, linen is better for drying glassware, dishes, and utensils. Dish towels of 100 percent linen will become softer and more supple with use and washing. One downside: linen is more vulnerable to mildew, so make sure to lay towels flat or hang to dry after each use.

35 Organizing less-used items

Store specialty utensils in a drawer equipped with dividers. A two-tiered tray will double drawer space and further separate utensils by frequency of use. Put popular utensils such as a can opener, vegetable peeler, and measuring spoons on the top tier and less-used items (the candy thermometer, melon baller, and turkey baster) on the bottom.

QUICK TIP: **S Hooks**

Instead of a crock crammed full of utensils, consider mounting a stainless-steel bar on the wall behind the sink, the backsplash, or on the side of a cabinet and dangle utensils from S hooks on the bar.

36   Three ways to store knives

1. Knife block. If counter space permits, knife blocks are a convenient and safe way to store knives. They are designed to protect blades from nicks and dulling, and keep knives within easy reach.

2. Magnetic knife strip. This stylish alternative saves both counter and drawer space and provides the best visibility. Look for one with a strong magnetic grip that also releases easily when you grasp the handle. For safety, mount it out of the way, such as behind a counter, and never on the side of an island or anyplace where knives might be accidentally bumped off the strip.

3. Horizontal drawer organizer. If you are going to store knives in a drawer, do so with a horizontal organizer to prevent them from knocking up against one another, which can damage the blades and potentially nick the fingers reaching for them.

37 One-Hour Project
Clean out the fridge

1. Temporarily crank up the coolness control, since the door will be open for longer than usual. Make note of the original setting.

2. Take all food and condiments out of the fridge.

3. Throw away food that has gone bad, expired, grown fuzz, or that you no longer use.

4. Remove shelves and crisper drawers and scrub them thoroughly in the sink.

5. Add a half cup of baking soda to a bucket of hot water to make an odor-free natural cleaner that is perfectly safe to use around food. (You definitely don't want to use harsh chemical cleaners for this.)

6. Dampen a cloth with the baking soda solution and wipe clean all surfaces inside the fridge.

7. Clean nonremovable storage areas such as the butter and egg compartments.

8. Rinse the fridge again with clean water and a clean rag to remove the baking soda solution.

9. Wipe down jars of food and other sticky surfaces.

10. Put the food back in the fridge (see entry 38, "How to organize the fridge").

11. Open a fresh box of baking soda to absorb future odors.

12. Reset the temperature control to its original setting.

38   How to organize the fridge

1. Keep like items together.

2. Open only one bottle of each condiment at a time. Try to limit them to the door, but if there are too many, contain them by category using a clear plastic bin.

3. Reposition shelves, if possible, to accommodate taller groceries.

4. Put taller items in back (where you can see them).

5. If your fridge is short on crisper drawers, clear plastic stackable containers are perfect for grouping smaller similar items together such as cheeses or lunch meat.

6. Don't overstock.

7. Use drawers as intended by the manufacturer, since they are climate controlled to extend the shelf life of the foods they are meant to contain.

8. Use stackable clear square containers (a more efficient use of space than round). To save even more space, use the smallest container possible to store leftovers.

9. Use one crisper drawer for produce requiring the highest humidity only (90 to 100 percent) such as beans, berries, broccoli, celery, cucumbers, and leafy green vegetables.

10. Use the other produce drawer creatively.

    a. kids snacks—pudding, yogurt, snack-size bags of baby carrots and precut celery sticks (down low where kids can reach them)

    b. drinks—bottled water, juice, beer, or soda

    c. naughty foods (out of sight, out of mind?)

39   Fruits and vegetables— refrigerate or not?

Proper storage can extend the shelf life of fruits and vegetables. Follow these guidelines:

Location	Fruits & Melons		Vegetables	

In refrigerator	apples
	(if storing more than 7 days)
	apricots
	blackberries
	blueberries
	cherries
	cut fruit
	figs
	grapes
	raspberries
	strawberries
			artichokes
			asparagus
			green beans
			lima beans
			beets
			Belgian endive
			broccoli
			brussels
			  sprouts
			cabbage
			carrots
			cauliflower
			celery
			cut vegetables
			green onions
				herbs
				  (except basil)
				leafy
				  vegetables
				leeks
				lettuce
				mushrooms
				peas
				radishes
				spinach
				sprouts
				summer
				  squashes
				sweet corn

Ripen on the counter first, then store in the refrigerator	avocados kiwifruit nectarines	peaches pears plums		

Store only at room temperature	apples (fewer
	  than 7 days)
	bananas
	cantaloupe
	grapefruit
	lemons
	limes
	mandarins
	mangoes
		oranges
		papayas
		persimmons
		pineapple
		plantains
		pomegran-
		  ates
		watermelons
			basil (in water)
			cucumbers
			dry onions
			eggplant
			garlic
			ginger
			jicama
			peppers
			potatoes
			pumpkins
				sweet
				  potatoes
				tomatoes
				winter
				  squashes

Chart reprinted courtesy of UC Davis Postharvest Technology (http://postharvest.ucdavis.edu)

what's a disorganized person to do?

- Store garlic, onions, potatoes, and sweet potatoes in a well-ventilated area in the pantry. Protect potatoes from light to avoid greening.
- Cucumbers, eggplant, and peppers can be kept in the refrigerator for 1 to 3 days if they are used soon after removal from the refrigerator.

QUICK TIP: **Supermarket Wisdom**

If produce is not in the refrigerated section of the grocery store, don't keep it in the fridge at home.

40   How to use crisper drawers

Crisper drawers regulate temperature and humidity to maximize the life of produce. But since you can't easily see what's in there, these compartments are often the place where good food becomes rotten and forgotten. As a rule of thumb, use crisper drawers as they are designated by the manufacturer, but rather than stuffing all your produce in the crisper drawers, use them for the fruits and vegetables requiring highest humidity (90 to 100 percent) and coolest temperature (32 to 40°F): beans, berries, broccoli, celery, cucumbers, and leafy green vegetables. Other produce will survive just fine in other parts of the fridge.

41 Garlic and potatoes, onions and tomatoes

- Garlic, onions, and potatoes should be stored in a cool, dry, dark place with good air circulation, never in plastic bags. A two- or three-tiered vegetable stand inside the pantry is ideal and can accommodate other vegetables like sweet potatoes and winter squash as well.
- Garlic, onions, and potatoes can be stored in a drawer next to the stove. As long as the drawer doesn't get too hot, the produce keeps well and makes food preparation a breeze.
- Tomatoes should be kept at room temperature away from direct sunlight (which causes uneven ripening). Refrigerated tomatoes turn mealy and lose their flavor.
- To ripen tomatoes, set them aside in a loosely folded brown paper bag at room temperature for about one to two days. This works for all fruit that ripens and/or sweetens after picking, such as peaches, plums, avocados, pears, cantaloupe, and bananas. To ripen fruit faster, add an apple to the bag. Apples emit ethylene gas, which, when trapped in a paper bag, speeds the ripening process.

42 Diagnosis: condimentia

Common, yet curable. Chronic condimentia sufferers are likely to accumulate inappropriate quantities of sauces and salad dressings. Other symptoms include forgetting about the half-empty jars of jam and jelly and opening a second or even a third. If left untreated, condimentia will lead to a hostile takeover of the fridge by mustards, mayos, and marinades.

The 5-step cure

1. Locate multiple jars of capers, ketchups, and conserves, discard any past their prime, and consolidate the rest. If you still have more than one of a particular condiment, use the oldest first and store the other(s) together in the *back* of the fridge in a container such as a plastic carton. Always check this container before you open any new condiment.

2. Store unopened condiments that don't require refrigeration in the pantry until you need them.

3. Keep like with like. Categorize by spicy (hot sauces, chili powder), sweet (jam, honey, maple syrup), savory (mayo, ketchup, mustard, pesto), and salad dressings.

4. If condiments tend to expire before you finish them, buy smaller bottles.

5. Limit your condiment collection to the shelves of the fridge door.

43 When to toss: condiments

Most condiments are stamped with a USE BY date. The following chart can also help to assess whether your condiments are past their prime.

Condiment	Unopened	Opened*
KETCHUP	1 year	6 months
MAYONNAISE	10–12 months	3–4 months after date on package
MUSTARD	2 years	1 year
OLIVE OIL	2 years	18–24 months
SALAD DRESSING (SOLD UNREFRIGERATED)	12–18 months	6–9 months
SALAD DRESSING (SOLD REFRIGERATED)	6 months	6 months or date on package
SOY SAUCE	3 years	2 years
TERIYAKI SAUCE	2 years	2 years
WORCESTERSHIRE SAUCE	3 years	2 years

Source: StillTasty (stilltasty.com)

* With refrigeration

44 What's the best way to unpack groceries

In the checkout line at the grocery store, take frozen and refrigerated items out of the cart first and ask the checkout person to bag them together in one or two bags. This way, you can unpack these bags immediately when you get home. When unpacking nonperishables, if counter space permits, unpack groceries and group similar items together on the countertop so you can make fewer trips to the pantry, bathroom, and other storage areas.

45 Organizing frozen food

Containment, coding, and labeling are key.

- Store leftovers in square, stackable clear plastic containers. Label each leftover container with the contents and a "use by" date, and rotate older items forward as you add new ones.
- Keep like items such as packages of frozen fruit and vegetables together in freezer bins or simple plastic baskets.
- Color-code freezer bins (or baskets) with colored dot stickers. Green means vegetables, red for meat, yellow for chicken, etc.
- Stack frozen meals with labels facing out.
- The door is the warmest part of the freezer, so store juice, butter, or frozen waffles there, but never meat.

46   Do I need a stand-alone freezer?

Stand-alone freezers are a must for anyone who buys or cooks in bulk. There are two types: uprights and top loaders. Upright freezers have doors that open like a refrigerator and come with shelves and storage drawers. Top-loading chests are best for storing large and bulky food items such as meats. Chests are harder to organize than uprights; lift-out drawers and sliding baskets make it easier to organize food. Mount a dry-erase board on the outside to keep an inventory of what's stored inside. That way, you'll always know what's on hand as well as what needs to be replenished.

Food	How long (months)
MEAT (ROASTS, STEAKS & CHOPS)	4–12
MEAT (GROUND)	3–4
MEAT (COOKED)	2–3
POULTRY (WHOLE)	12
POULTRY (PARTS)	9
POULTRY (GIBLETS)	3–4
POULTRY (COOKED)	4
FISH	3–6
BUTTER	6–9
MILK	3*
ICE CUBES	3–4**

*Thaw in fridge and double-check freshness with smell test.
**Ice is safe to use beyond this time, but will absorb odors to give it an off taste.

47 How to de-clutter the outside of the fridge

- Put photos of family, friends, and Fido in clear plastic magnetic photo frames (sold at photo stores) to prevent edges from curling and to give a neatened overall appearance.
- Use 8 x 10-inch magnetic photo frames for larger items such as emergency contact lists, fitness-class schedules, school calendars, and kids' extracurricular activity schedules.
- As a way to keep multiple contact lists, schedules, and calendars easily accessible, hole-punch the top left corner of important papers and dangle them from a magnetic hook.
- Ask your young artist(s) to handpick one piece of art to display on the fridge at a time. Rotate artwork weekly.

QUICK TIP: **Choopa Board**

Choopa Board is a powder-coated sheet of metal with powerful suction cups that grip the slick, nonmagnetized surface of glass, granite, or stainless-steel appliances, turning a section of a fridge into a magnetized surface. Available at www.choopaboard.com.

If you are willing to make a minimal investment for new plastic food storage containers, recycle or donate your old ones and buy only two sizes, small and large. This way, all of your containers will nest to perfection and take up the least amount of space in your cabinet. Plus, you will have to choose between only two lid sizes, saving time as well as space!

48 How to organize food storage containers

Almost everyone is guilty of hoarding far more plastic containers than they actually ever use at once. Managing their rate of accumulation will ensure that they don't take over the kitchen.

• Save the best. Keep sets of containers, which are made to nest. Square, transparent containers fit snugly next to one another so they use space more efficiently than round ones. Choose transparent containers so you can see what's inside.

• Get rid of the rest. Unless you have a specific use for them, give away or recycle packaging containers such as cream cheese or margarine tubs. Throw out warped, melted, or otherwise damaged containers or containers with missing or ill-fitting lids.

• Nest the remaining containers by size on an assigned shelf or drawer.

• Use a basket to hold lids or store them upright by placing a dish rack or a napkin holder in the cabinet.

49   Feeding Pets

Decant dog and cat food into airtight containers to preserve freshness. Choose a container large enough to accommodate the contents of the bag you usually buy. If you have more than one type of food, instead of stacking bins with lids, try stackable bins with side access so that you don't have to move one bin to get to another. Store in a cool, dry place near food bowls and keep a scoop inside.

For feeding, choose bowls with nonskid rims or use an elevated feeding station to keep bowls in place and up off the floor. Elevated bowls aid in digestion and prevent strain on your pet's back and neck. Place near a wall to prevent tipping.

QUICK TIP: **Pet Medicine**

Keep all pet medications and ointments together and out of reach of children. Note dosage schedules on a family bulletin board or mark them on your calendar. Include your vet's phone number on your list of emergency numbers.

50 Getting your pantry in order

1. Take everything out of the pantry and wipe the shelves clean.

2. Check expiration dates and pitch anything expired, stale, or that you simply no longer use.

3. Group like things together and assign categories to shelves: keep soups with soups, cereals with cereals, etc.

4. Keep what you use most often on the shelves at eye level and easy to access.

5. Decant grains and legumes into uniform wide-mouth glass 16-ounce jars. Label the jars accordingly.

6. Install sliding pantry drawers for easy access to small items in the back.

7. Make use of the space on the back of the pantry door and hang a rack system, which can be customized and hung without tools. Various basket sizes can accommodate anything from small mix packets to two-liter soda bottles.

8. Maximize unused space between shelves, with shelf helpers such as under-shelf baskets and expanding shelves.

9. Use less accessible shelves for storing replacements of fridge items such as spare ketchup, mustard, jam, and salad dressing.

10. Store heavy items, such as bottled water and soda, on a low shelf or the floor. If you have additional space, you might also want to stash some less frequently used appliances here, too.

11. Use deep shelves for bulky items like paper towels.

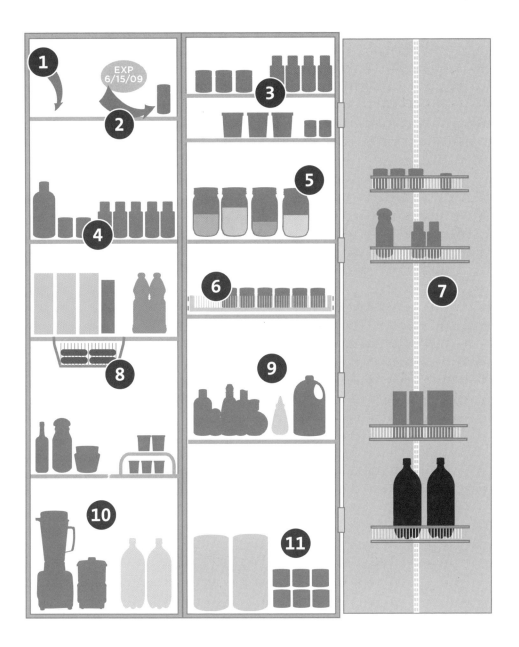

51　Storing grains and legumes

Since grains and legumes are sold in boxes and bags of all sizes, which doesn't make for easy storage, the trick is to buy what you need and repackage at home. Figure out what you consume and then buy enough wide-mouth 16-ounce jars to accommodate your needs. These jars have airtight screw tops that preserve the shelf life of grains and beans, keep bugs out, and stand neatly on a pantry shelf. Label the outside of the jars with a label maker.

52   Shelf life of grains and legumes

Grains and legumes, like most foods, are perishable. Extend their shelf lives by storing them in a cool, dark, and dry place. An airtight container will help retain freshness, protect against moisture, and keep out critters. Here's a guide to how long things keep.

Product	Shelf life
BARLEY	1 year
BEANS	1 year*
CHICKPEAS	1 year*
LENTILS	1 year*
MILLET	1 year
OATS	1 year (in humid environments, oats are best stored in the freezer)
QUINOA	1 year
RICE (WHITE)	Indefinitely when stored properly (airtight container in a cool, dry, dark cabinet)
RICE (BROWN)	1 month in pantry, 18 months in fridge or freezer (due to high oil content)
RYE	1 year
SPELT	1 year
WHEAT	1 year

Source: StillTasty (stilltasty.com)

*Storage time shown is for best quality. After that, texture, color, or flavor may change, but will most likely still be safe to consume if stored properly.

the kitchen

57

53   Storing spices: five solutions

Many freestanding spice racks are available, but unless you have unlimited counter space, try one of these space-saving options. Regardless of what method you choose, alphabetizing spices is the best way to find what you are looking for.

1. Wall. Hang a spice rack on the wall.

2. Drawer. For a fairly deep drawer near the stove, use a drawer insert that holds spices with the labels facing up. Or stand spices up, labeling the jar tops with a label maker.

3. Cabinet. Mount a spice cabinet on a cabinet door. Check dimensions so that the spice shelves clear the cabinet shelves, allowing the door to close.

4. Indian spice box. Made of stainless steel (usually measuring seven to nine inches), an Indian spice box contains seven round compartments along with a measure. A proper spice box has a tight-fitting inner lid between the lid and the compartments so that the spices don't mix. Fill the compartments with your favorites, and avoid having to open multiple spice canisters while cooking. You can display the spice box on the counter if space permits, or just bring it out when cooking. Spice boxes are available in any Indian market or online (search for "masala daani").

5. Mason jars. Buying in bulk is a great way to save money on spices you cycle through quickly. If you store opened bags of bulk spices together, stronger spices will affect milder ones, so it's best to contain them separately. Small Mason or canning jars work well. They make efficient use of cabinet space and can be stacked. Transfer spices from the bags they came in to airtight pint-size (or larger) jars with twist-off lids. Label the side of the jar and stack in the cabinet or on a shelf with labels facing forward.

54 One-Hour Project
Make your own magnetized spice canisters

Housewares stores carry magnetic spice canisters, but doing it yourself is easy and less expensive.

1. Count up the spices you'd like to store and buy the corresponding number of magnetic storage tins.

2. Print labels using a label maker and adhere the labels to the sides of the tins or simply write the name of the spice with a fine-point indelible ink marker on the back of the container. Labeling the *lid* can result in confusion if you take off more than one lid at a time.

3. Remove the glass lids and transfer each spice into its respective tin, using a funnel to avoid spills. Replace the glass lids.

4. Arrange the finished product on the front or side of the refrigerator or on any magnetized surface (such as a magnetic knife strip) away from the heat of the stove and direct sunlight.

55   When to toss: spices

Spices don't go bad; they just lose their oomph. To check their strength, just crush them between your fingers and smell. If you smell nothing, your spices are done. If the smell is weak, use them up fast, doubling the amount a recipe calls for, or just chuck them and start fresh. Ground spices such as allspice or cumin typically last eight months to three years, while leafy herbs such as thyme and oregano retain their potency for one to three years. When you buy a new spice, record the date on the side of the bottle or tin. Always seal tightly after each use. For maximum value and freshness, buy whole spices and grind them as needed with a mortar and pestle or a coffee grinder dedicated to spices. If stored properly, whole spices will retain their potency for up to four years. Aromatic whole spices such as cardamom, cloves, and cumin stay fresh longer than that; and cinnamon, whole peppercorns, and nutmeg will last even longer.

56   Storing everyday wineglasses

For casual-use stemware, mount an undershelf hanging stemware rack to help prevent the lips of the glasses from chipping. If your cupboard shelves are adjustable, place the shelf high enough so that there will be enough space to store other items below the glasses without knocking into them. Or move the shelf to a lower level so that there is no wasted space beneath the glasses. If you choose to keep stemware on a cabinet shelf, place every other glass upside down to maximize space.

the kitchen

57 Caring for crystal stemware

To prevent chips and scratches on fine crystal, keep it out of contact with other stemware or dishes. Store infrequently used items in a stemware storage box with padded dividers to prevent glasses from knocking up against one another. Keep crystal stemware right side up to avoid putting stress on glass rims. Avoid storing crystal in extreme temperatures. Always wash crystal by hand, using a mild soap. Never twist the stem while washing, and be sure to put a rubber mat in the bottom of the sink to prevent chipping. As a final rinse, add a cup of vinegar to a sinkful of warm water for a nonresidue, spot-free shine.

QUICK TIP: **Plate Protection**

Give fine china extra protection by enveloping individual plates in professional plastic food wrap, which is thicker and heavier than the standard variety and available at most warehouse clubs. Stack up to eight and then wrap the entire stack in plastic, too, to secure plates and protect them from dust and scratches.

58 How to store fine china

Store fine china in padded china storage bags with dividers to protect against scratches, dust, and breakage. Stack same-size plates on top of one another and lay felt plate protectors between each to prevent chipping or scratching. Choose china storage bags with identification windows or ID tags on the outside, using a label maker to label the contents. Many china storage bag sets accommodate a full service of twelve. Store the china storage bags on a low shelf or in a hutch to make them easier to retrieve and put back (and more likely to survive an earthquake). Always keep china at room temperature;

never store it in the garage or attic, where extreme heat or cold could cause cracking. Store creamers, sugar bowls, teapots, and other nonstackable pieces on a felt-lined cabinet shelf with ample space between them. Invert lids, rest them on the base, and place a piece of felt in between the two pieces. Never stack cups, as stacking makes them vulnerable to chipping.

QUICK TIP: **Not Just for Chalkboards**

Store sterling silver with a piece of white chalk, which will absorb moisture and delay tarnishing.

59   Keeping your good silver

Storing sterling silver properly will prevent scratching, minimize tarnishing, and ensure a long life with less need for upkeep. Silver is best stored in a cloth case treated with an antitarnish agent that absorbs tarnish-producing gases in the air such as sulfur compounds. For further protection, place the wrapped silver in a clear plastic Mylar or polyethylene bag. Storing silver in this way will reduce the need for cleaning and polishing. Choose a cool, dry place free of humidity or moisture to store the bags.

60   Dishwasher ins and outs

Loading

- Scrape plates before loading but don't prewash dishes, which wastes water and hinders dishwashing detergent's ability to attack food particles that cling to dirty dishes.
- Load glasses, stemware, and plastic containers on the dishwasher top rack for lower water pressure and cooler temperature. Stronger pressure on the bottom can break glass and melt or warp plastic.
- Putting glasses in the rows between the prongs rather than over the prongs will keep them more secure and prevent chipping.
- Load plates by size to make unloading easier.
- Load silverware into the caddy with the useful end—especially fork tines and knife blades—up. Some, however, think that grabbing handles when unloading is both safer and more hygienic.
- Mix up silverware. Some will argue that loading silverware by type makes unloading quicker, but nesting forks and spooning spoons won't get cleaned.

Unloading

- Open the door as soon as the dishwasher shuts off. This allows remaining moisture to escape. Hot dishes steam away moisture and dry more quickly—usually within about ten minutes.
- If your dishwasher is not performing up to par, check for food particles clogging the mechanical parts in the base. Remove any debris.
- Empty the bottom rack first so that little pools of water in the bottom of mugs and glasses on the top rack won't drip onto dishes below.
- Take the silverware caddy with you to the silverware drawer.

- Rather than putting dishes in the cabinet one by one, unload them into stacks (by size) on the counter and then put the stacks away. Store dishware close to the dishwasher for ease in unloading.
- Unload promptly so dirty dishes don't pile up in the sink.

What *not* to put in the dishwasher

While most dishes, glasses, and kitchen tools are dishwasher-safe, over time the effects of heat, detergent, and water pressure can do their damage. Hand wash anything you cherish or want to preserve. The following items are generally better off with hand washing:

- Stainless steel. Though dishwasher-safe, stainless pots and pans will last longer with hand washing.
- Cast iron. Never put in the dishwasher, as detergent will strip away the seasoned surface and cause rust.
- Aluminum. Hand wash all aluminum unless it's designated dishwasher-safe.
- Wood. The heat and steam of a dishwasher's dry cycle can warp wood, so take care to hand wash wood utensils, cutting boards, and serving dishes, including wood-handled items.
- Antique or hand-painted china. While some new fine china is dishwasher-safe, most antique dishes can be damaged in the dishwasher.
- Plastic. High heat can warp plastic. If a plastic item isn't guaranteed dishwasher-safe by the manufacturer, hand wash it. If you do put plastic in the dishwasher, place it in the upper tray.
- Knives. Though many knives are generally safe to put in the dishwasher, most manufacturers recommend hand washing them with warm water and a little detergent, rinsing and then drying immediately with a towel. Also, be aware that knocking against other items in the silverware basket can dull the blade, so you may have to resharpen more often.

61 Cabinet rehab

Chances are that your base cabinets, because of their proximity to the floor, hold heavier kitchen items such as pots, pans, and less frequently used appliances. If you don't mind getting down on your knees to locate something in the back, your system is working. If not, rehabilitate your cabinets with a mountable drawer system, which brings everything from the back into plain view. Home improvement and organization stores and their Web sites feature a wide selection of gliding pull-out cabinets that are easy to install.

62 How to avoid the "cabinet shuffle"

If getting to what you need in your cabinet involves endless rearranging, try stepped shelving. Plastic or metal stepped shelves don't necessarily create more space, but they bring canned goods, spices, etc., into full view by elevating items in the back, so that you can see what's there. The expandable variety can be sized to fit any cabinet. If you are a do-it-yourself type, cut two-by-fours to fit the width of your cabinet and stair step them to create the same effect.

QUICK TIP: **Extend Your Reach**

If a high shelf is just beyond your reach, and getting out the stepladder is too much effort, keep a foam yoga block under the kitchen sink and use it as a step. They are lightweight and unobtrusive, and you will gain four to six inches—just enough to grab that coffee grinder.

63   Ten under-cabinet space savers

1. Mounted appliances (microwave, coffeemaker, toaster)

2. Utility hooks for coffee mugs

3. Paper towel rod

4. Stemware rack

5. Dish towel holder

6. Narrow shelf for place mats and table linens

7. Cookbook holder

8. Wall-mounted spice rack

9. Task lighting

10. Banana hook (prevents bananas bruising and helps them ripen evenly)

64 Island life

If the kitchen is the heart of the home, then the island is the heartbeat. A kitchen island serves a multitude of functions besides being a place to prepare food. Among other things, the island is a place where kids hang out to do homework or make art. An organized island is one that sustains the life that happens there. In addition to storing small appliances, bakeware, and other kitchen gadgetry in the drawers and cabinets of the island, dedicate a low drawer for coloring books, crayons, construction paper, safety scissors, and glue; in another drawer keep homework supplies like a calculator, ruler, notebook paper, and pens and pencils.

65 When to toss: pots and pans

Most people have more pots and pans than they actually need or use. Here's what you can eliminate right now:

• Duplicates. If you have more than one in a particular size, save the best one and donate the rest.
• Anything rusty, broken, or burnt
• Worn or pitted aluminum cookware
• Nonstick pots and pans (see entry 68, "Do you stick with nonstick?")

66   Caring for pots and pans

Stainless steel. Hand wash in warm, soapy water using a nonabrasive cleanser and a dishcloth or sponge. For baked-on food, soak the pot in hot water for 30 to 60 minutes and then put back on the stove and boil for 10 to 15 minutes. Let the water cool, and then scrub the pot with a nylon-net scouring pad or a brush made of nylon or plastic. Avoid steel wool or metal scouring pads as these will scratch the surface. To remove water stains, scrub the spots gently with baking soda or, for rust and tougher stains, use Bar Keepers Friend. Do not store salty or acidic foods in stainless steel because these can corrode cookware. Though most stainless steel is generally safe to put in the dishwasher, hand washing will guarantee a longer life.

Cast iron. Season new cast-iron cookware before use to create a nonstick surface and prevent rust. Preheat the oven to 300°F. Wash the pan in hot, soapy water and hand dry immediately. Lightly coat the pan with vegetable oil and then bake the pan in the oven (on the center shelf) for an hour. Remove and let cool for 1 to 2 hours and then wipe any excess oil off with a paper towel. James Peterson, in *What's a Cook to Do?*, states that "ideally cast iron should be cleaned only by wiping with a dish towel or paper towel. If you need to wash it with soap and water, you'll need to reseason it." Whatever you do, avoid abrasive scouring pads and cleansers and wipe dry right away. If rust appears, remove it with steel wool and reseason. Store cast iron with lids off to keep moisture out and prevent future rust. Do not store food in cast iron as it produces a metallic taste. When stacking cast-iron with other pots and pans, place a paper towel in between to protect the seasoning.

Enameled cast iron. Though dishwasher safe, repeated dishwasher use will dull the enamel, so best to hand wash. Allow to cool before washing and then hand wash in hot soapy water. Rinse with warm water and then dry immediately. For stubborn food particles, fill with warm water and let soak for 15 to 20 minutes and then wash as usual. Nylon scrubbing pads are okay to use but avoid metallic scouring pads and harsh abrasive cleansers, which will damage the enamel. Use only silicone, wood, or plastic utensils.

Aluminum. Hand wash to avoid staining and dry immediately. To avoid scratching, use only wooden, plastic, or smooth metal cooking utensils. To remove baked-on food, fill the pan with water and simmer over low heat to loosen burnt-on food particles. Let cool and scour with a nylon-net scouring pad. Rinse as usual. Use a mild detergent when possible. Even baking soda may discolor aluminum so before using a stronger cleaner, pretest a hidden surface to make sure it doesn't damage the pan.

Ceramics. Nonporous, chip-resistant stoneware can withstand high temperatures, and is dishwasher safe. Earthenware, which is porous, prone to chipping, and cannot stand high temperatures, should be hand washed. To find out how to tell the difference, visit Seeley's Stoneware (http://stoneware.seeleys.com) and click on the "What Is Stoneware" link. Ceramic knives are safe to put in the dishwasher, but blades are prone to chipping if they knock against hard objects.

Nonstick. Wash with a dishcloth in hot, soapy water. Avoid abrasive cleansers or pads and use only nylon, plastic, or wood utensils when cooking, as metal will damage the nonstick finish. Allow the pan to cool before washing. (See also entry 68, "Do you stick with nonstick?")

67 Storing cookware

In the cabinet

Store pots and pans in cabinets near the stove. The most convenient way to store cookware in a cabinet is to equip the cabinet with sliding pull-out shelves. (See entry 61, "Cabinet rehab.") Slide-out drawers reduce the need to nest pots and pans, so you can grab what you need without having to move the whole stack. If cabinet space is limited, store seldom-used pots in another location (such as the pantry or garage).

In very small spaces

For extremely limited space, try stackable pots and pans with detachable handles.

Hanging from the ceiling

Hanging pots and pans from the ceiling puts unused space to use and frees up cabinets. Ceiling pot racks come in a variety of shapes and sizes. A rectangular pot rack might fit quite well in a long,

rectangular kitchen with an island. If your kitchen is small, try a square or circular rack, which takes up less space. While pots are usually hung facing front to back, which makes them easier to see and reach, pot racks are available for hanging pots sideways so they can nest, thus taking up less space. Make sure pots have handles that can be hung from a hook, and be sure to buy hooks and hardware that will support the weight of your pots.

Hanging on the wall

There are many wall-mounted pot racks on the market. Some even come with a built-in shelf to hold cookbooks or stockpots. A towel bar with S hooks mounted on the wall takes up even less space. Or

take a page from Julia Child, who hung her pots and pans on a Peg-Board wall. Use assorted hooks for different size items and reposition them until you've created a configuration that is functional and appealing to the eye. (Julia actually traced the shapes of pots and pans onto the Peg-Board to make it easy to return an implement to its rightful spot.) You can cover an entire wall or just hang a small square painted in a bright color to add a design element to the kitchen.

the kitchen

71

68 Do you stick with nonstick?

Are nonstick pans safe? According to Margaret Shield, coordinator of the Toxic-Free Legacy Coalition in Washington State, this is what we currently know:

- Perfluorooctanoic acid (PFOA), the chemical used in nonstick coating, is a likely human carcinogen.
- When heated, nonstick coating releases small amounts of PFOA particles and gases into the air. Pet birds have an acute response to these vapors and often die when Teflon pans are used in the home.
- PFOA has been found to cause cancer, organ damage, and birth defects in animals. Human risk is still unknown, but the more research done on PFOA, the more we learn of its toxicity.

The manufacture, use, and disposal of PFOA products has been shown to pose an environmental and health risk because these long-lived toxic chemicals continue to build up in our bodies, the environment, and in wildlife over time. To reduce risk, the Toxic-Free Legacy Coalition recommends stainless steel, cast-iron, or enameled cast-iron cookware.

69 Four ways to store pot lids

Pot lids are easily one of the hardest kitchen items to control. They don't nest, stack, or stand on end. People tend to store pot lids with pots, but the key is to treat them as their own category and organize them accordingly. Here are four ways to tame them:

1. Drawer. If possible, dedicate a deep drawer to lids. The storage drawer underneath a built-in oven is a great spot because its width makes what you're looking for easy to find.

2. Basket. Put a basket on a cabinet shelf and pull it out to find the lid you need. There are also mountable sliding baskets for lids.

3. Rack. A pot lid rack can be mounted inside a cabinet door.

4. Improvise. Install a stainless steel towel rack on the wall behind the stove for your most-often-used lids.

 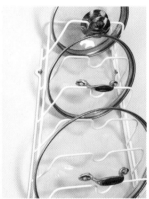

70   How to organize bakeware

You've probably noticed that pie pans, muffin tins, and other bakeware don't nest well, and no one likes taking everything out of the cabinet to get to the cookie sheet at the bottom of the pile. The solution is to stack bakeware vertically, outfitting a cabinet with vertical partitions. Divide a cabinet with rows of small spring-tension curtain rods placed vertically in the front and back of the cabinet (with about four to six inches in between); bakeware can stand on edge and lean up against the rods.

71 Waffle irons and other kitchen gadgets

A kitchen island is a good place to store seldom-used appliances or seasonal cookware. If space is limited, however, look elsewhere in the house for places to keep occasional-use appliances and pots. A top or bottom shelf in a reach-in or walk-in pantry is one option. Or store them on a wire-shelving unit in the basement or garage. Be sure to cover appliances to protect them from dust. The space between the upper cabinets and the ceiling is an often-overlooked storage place. If appliances are attractive enough, they can be kept here in full view; if not, they can be concealed in matching baskets.

72 Organizing table linens

Unlike bedsheets, long linen tablecloths should not be folded into tight bundles and stored on shelves. Instead, fold them lengthwise and hang over two wooden hangers on a closet rod or a hook on the back of the linen closet door. Protect the linen from the wood by draping a few sheets of acid-free paper over the hangers, which will also provide padding at the point of the fold. Cover them with another sheet to protect against dust, which can damage the fabric. If there isn't room in the linen closet, hang them on a closet rod in a guest bedroom or other closet.

73 Cataloging cookbooks

Organizing cookbooks will depend a lot on the size of your collection and the available bookshelf space in the kitchen and elsewhere. First, sort cookbooks based on their frequency of use: weekly, monthly, occasionally, never. Cookbooks that are used weekly should go on a shelf in the kitchen. If you don't have a built-in shelf for books, removing a cabinet door can make it look as if you do. Or use available wall space to hang a shelf or even a pot rack with a shelf on top. For other cookbooks, consider how many recipes you actually use from each. If only one or two, consider scanning these and donating the book. Look for unused space in or near the kitchen such as the top of cabinets, to house books you use more often. Donate cookbooks that you never use. Arrange cookbooks by cuisine (such as Italian, Indian, Mexican, California, French) and general topics (such as soups, baking, vegetarian, desserts).

Creating an online catalog

The LibraryThing Web site (www.librarything.com) allows you to create a library-quality catalog of your cookbooks. You can catalog up to two hundred for free, but a small fee entitles you to a lifetime membership and unlimited entries. (You can eventually catalog the rest of your book collection, too.) Adding books to the catalog is fast and easy. Just type in a few words of the title, and LibraryThing fills in the rest of the data from more than 690 libraries around the world, including the Library of Congress, and Amazon. Once your catalog is set up, you can sort, search, and edit your collection as well as add tags to search by cuisine or topic. You can also add tags that identify where a book is located in your home, so you'll always be able to find it. You can even access your catalog with your cell phone (if it has a browser) while in a bookstore. LibraryThing also allows users to share reviews and connect to others with similar libraries, as well as offering alerts about local book signings and events.

QUICK TIP: **Recipe Tag**

Instead of separating new recipes you want to try from your other recipes, keep them in the same filing system and tag them with one-inch Post-it flags on which you can jot down TRY ME or other notes.

74   Recipe keeping

Regardless of how you choose to organize your recipes, you'll want a system that enables you to easily find the recipe you are looking for, add new recipes, browse for ideas, and keep recipe cards splatter- and grease-free. You'll also want to divide your recipes into categories that make sense to you. If you aren't sure about which categories to create, check the contents of a favorite cookbook and start with those. You can always create more categories or subdivisions if necessary.

1. Box. A recipe box is often a prized family heirloom, especially if it contains handwritten family recipes in a mother's or grandmother's hand. The one downside to the traditional recipe box is its small capacity. Today, when we have access to so many different types of ingredients and recipes, our repertoire has increased, and so have our storage needs. A photo-organizing box has more space than a traditional recipe box. *A* to *Z* dividers let you order recipes alphabetically, or flip them around to write in your own categories on the tabs.

2. Binder. Organize recipes into two- or three-inch binders. Putting each recipe into a three-hole-punched clear plastic sheet protector makes browsing easier and also keeps recipes clean. Binders are

great for organizing recipes that you print off the computer. If the recipe is cut out from a periodical or is written on the front of an index card, you may want to glue it to a blank sheet of paper before putting it in plastic. Separate categories with subject dividers and label the divider tabs with a label maker or pen. One client who did a lot of baking made two binders—one for cooking and one for baking.

3. File. With a label maker, print category labels for the partitions in an accordian folder. Insert a manila folder labeled with the category so you can pull the whole file out and easily return it when you are done.

75 Computerizing recipes

Digitize your collection with cookbook and recipe organizing software such as BigOven, eChefs, and MasterCook Deluxe. Many of these can also help create weekly or monthly menus, keep an inventory of ingredients, create shopping lists organized by aisle, and estimate your grocery bill. Better yet, cut digital clutter completely and go virtual, by using an online recipe database. Often these allow you to compile a "recipe box" of your favorites, search by ingredient, send recipes to your cell phone, and even create your own printed cookbooks.

Cookstr.com compiles recipes from the best cookbook authors and well-known chefs. Fueled by a dynamic search engine, Cookstr.com lets you look up recipes according to different search guidelines, such as "one-pot meals" or "short preparation times."

QUICK TIP: **Keeping Recipe Cards Clean**

While cooking or baking, place your recipe index card in a Ziploc bag to keep it clean.

the kitchen

76 One-Hour Project
A customized shopping list

1. Go through your refrigerator, freezer, pantry, kitchen cabinets, bathroom cabinets, shower, laundry room, etc., and make a list of all foods and products that you and your family use regularly.

2. Group them by categories so that you can shop efficiently, aisle by aisle, without having to repeatedly look up and down your entire shopping list. Possible categories are: fresh fruits and vegetables, frozen foods, dairy items, snacks, paper goods, cleaning supplies, and beauty supplies. Add a few blank lines in each category for special-occasion items.

3. Type the list on the computer and save it. Print out multiple copies and keep them in a file in or near the kitchen.

4. Keep one copy of the list on the refrigerator so that when you run low on something, you can check it off. When you are ready to go shopping, your list will already be made for you.

5. Remember to bring the list!

FRUIT
- ❏ apples
- ❏ bananas
- ❏ pears
- ❏ oranges
- ❏ grapes
- ❏ berries
- ❏ lemons
- ❏ limes
- ❏ mangoes
- ❏ _____
- ❏ _____
- ❏ _____

DRINKS
- ❏ sparkling water
- ❏ soda
- ❏ orange juice
- ❏ apple juice
- ❏ juice boxes
- ❏ soy milk
- ❏ coffee
- ❏ tea
- ❏ _____
- ❏ _____
- ❏ _____

CONDIMENTS
- ❏ olive oil
- ❏ balsamic vinegar
- ❏ jam
- ❏ nut butter
- ❏ mustard
- ❏ ketchup
- ❏ salad dressing
- ❏ maple syrup
- ❏ honey
- ❏ _____
- ❏ _____
- ❏ _____

VEGETABLES
- ❏ salad greens
- ❏ carrots
- ❏ cucumbers
- ❏ tomatoes
- ❏ potatoes
- ❏ avacado
- ❏ broccoli
- ❏ squash
- ❏ garlic
- ❏ onions
- ❏ _____
- ❏ _____
- ❏ _____

DAIRY
- ❏ milk
- ❏ cheese
- ❏ eggs
- ❏ butter
- ❏ cream cheese
- ❏ yogurt
- ❏ sour cream
- ❏ cottage cheese
- ❏ _____
- ❏ _____

CLEANING SUPPLIES
- ❏ sponges
- ❏ dishwashing liquid
- ❏ hand soap
- ❏ all-purpose cleaner
- ❏ drain declogger
- ❏ laundry detergent
- ❏ fabric softener
- ❏ glass cleaner
- ❏ _____
- ❏ _____
- ❏ _____

BREAKFAST
- ❏ oatmeal
- ❏ oat bran flakes
- ❏ Cheerios
- ❏ granola
- ❏ _____
- ❏ _____

BREAD
- ❏ sliced bread
- ❏ pita bread
- ❏ English muffins
- ❏ tortillas
- ❏ bagels
- ❏ _____
- ❏ _____

PAPER & HOUSEHOLD
- ❏ paper towels
- ❏ napkins
- ❏ toilet paper
- ❏ tissues
- ❏ plastic wrap
- ❏ aluminum foil
- ❏ storage bags
- ❏ trash bags
- ❏ paper bags
- ❏ recycling bags
- ❏ straws
- ❏ lightbulbs
- ❏ _____

FROZEN FOOD
- ❏ frozen berries
- ❏ ice cream
- ❏ french fries
- ❏ pizza crusts
- ❏ _____
- ❏ _____
- ❏ _____

PACKAGED FOOD
- ❏ grains & beans
- ❏ pasta
- ❏ rice
- ❏ beans
- ❏ macaroni & cheese
- ❏ canned soups
- ❏ canned tuna fish
- ❏ _____
- ❏ _____

SNACKS
- ❏ nuts
- ❏ cookies
- ❏ chips
- ❏ salsa
- ❏ pretzels
- ❏ _____
- ❏ _____

SPICES
- ❏ salt
- ❏ pepper
- ❏ _____
- ❏ _____

PET SUPPLIES
- ❏ dog food
- ❏ cat food
- ❏ kitty litter
- ❏ treats
- ❏ _____

MISCELLANEOUS
- ❏ vitamins
- ❏ _____
- ❏ _____
- ❏ _____
- ❏ _____
- ❏ _____
- ❏ _____

78   Shopping at a warehouse club

Prior to leaving

- Organize your list. Know what you need and how much storage space you have.
- Invite a friend. To take advantage of bulk prices and savings, bring someone along with whom you can split large purchases.
- Bring plastic tubs. Since warehouse stores do not provide bags, bring a few plastic bins to contain loose items and transport purchases.

While shopping

- Know unit costs and price compare. Warehouse clubs can offer deep savings, but they do not accept manufacturer's coupons. Usually the best deals can be found on pantry items, over-the-counter medications, personal-care products, and big-ticket items such as electronics, appliances, and jewelry. Some smart phone applications can scan barcodes and find the best deals using Google product search.

Coming home

- Leave boxes behind. Avoid the hassle of disposing of boxes at home by bringing a box cutter with you to break down boxes as you load the car. Costco will collect and recycle empty boxes left behind in carts. Check with your local warehouse club to find out if it has similar recycling procedures.
- Unpack strategically. Keep similar items together when unloading into plastic bins. This will make unpacking at home much easier. For instance, keep frozen foods together to unpack them first. Keep paper goods in one tub and pantry items together in another.

79   How to organize take-out menus

Using a simple binder with plastic sleeves is better than throwing menus in a drawer. Use tabbed dividers to specify type of cuisine, such as Asian, Italian, Burgers, Deli, etc. To make ordering easy, highlight family members' most-requested dishes (and jot down any substitutions). Go through it once every six months and discard outdated or duplicated menus or ones from restaurants you didn't like.

80   Managing medications

Where to put pills
Medications are best stored in a cool, dry place—not in your bathroom's medicine cabinet where they can be damaged by humidity and temperature fluctuations. A kitchen cabinet (out of the reach of children) is a good solution. Store medicines by type, separating over-the-counter from prescription drugs. Stand medicine bottles upright (a portable container such as a lunch box will help keep them organized) and write the name of the prescription on a round label which can be adhered to the cap.

Your daily dose
If you are taking multiple medications, have a system in place to ensure you don't miss a dose.

QUICK TIP: **Magazine Keeping**

If you can't part with back issues of food magazines, organize them by month instead of title so that all holiday and seasonal recipes are grouped together.

the kitchen

- **Make a list.** Note all medications, including color of pill, dosage amount, time and frequency of the dose, and any additional instructions (TAKE WITH FOOD).
- **Organize pills.** On Sunday nights, refer to the list to dispense pills into a weekly pill organizer (available at most drugstores). If you take a considerable number of medications, buy *three* weekly pill organizers instead of one, labeling them MORNING, MIDDAY, and EVENING.
- **Keep medications together.** When you dispense pills every week, check vials to see which medications need to be refilled. Check expiration dates and the number of refills remaining, and call your doctor if your prescription needs an update.
- **Use reminders.** Set your cell phone, watch alarm, or computer to alert you that it's time to take your medications.

81   How to set up a kitchen bill-paying area

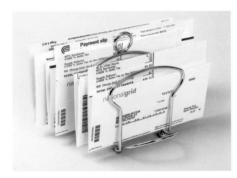

If you pay bills in the kitchen, the following systems will keep papers at bay, keep supplies at hand, and ensuretimely payments. If you don't already pay bills online, making the move to virtual banking will save you time and money and help the environment. (See entry 168, "Online bill-paying.") Two essential components are a place to put incoming bills and a place to store paid bills. If space permits, a thirty-two-slot bill organizer lets you organize bills by due date. Simply open bills when they arrive and file them in the numbered slot according to when they are due. A set of drawers is perfect for storing stamps, return address labels, and your checkbook. For smaller spaces, and a more elegant solution, use a toast caddy for incoming bills. Store paid bills in a twelve-month accordion file. Slots are labeled January through December. At the end of twelve months, when you get to the month in which you started, you can toss the bills for that month in the previous year, assuming you don't need to save them for tax purposes (see entry 173, "What do I save for taxes and for how long?"), so it's a constantly rotating system. This way, you'll always have the past year's (twelve months) statements available to you in a simple and self-contained system.

82   The Rolodex— relic or relevant?

While the Rolodex might seem like a dinosaur in today's digital world, it can be a valuable reference tool in the kitchen for making important household information available to others such as a housekeeper, babysitter, house sitter, subletter, or even a spouse or kids. For instance, make a Rolodex card for each major appliance such as the refrigerator, dishwasher, washing machine, dryer, etc. Include numbers to call for service and repair as well as serial numbers. This can be especially useful for arranging emergency repairs. On a card labeled PRINTER, write the model number of your printer. When you go to the store for replacement ink cartridges, you can readily jot down the info—or simply take the card with you. Do the same for vacuum bags and humidifier filters. Have a card labeled COMPUTER that lists tech support phone numbers and Web sites and your computer serial numbers. Make Rolodex cards for utilities such as the cable company and gas company (include account numbers on the card) as well as service people who come to the house such as the gardener and the handyman.

83 One-Hour Project
Take back the junk drawer

- Empty the entire drawer. If it comes out, turn it upside down to liberate the dirt that accumulates in the corners. Wipe the drawer clean.
- Throw away things that can actually be classified as "junk." Old soy sauce packets and inkless pens definitely qualify.
- Relocate anything that doesn't belong in the kitchen. Miscellaneous hardware and extra telephone/computer wires are better stored in a toolbox; safety pins and buttons in the sewing kit, and makeup in the bathroom. Designate a bowl or jar for change, rather than tossing it in the junk drawer.
- Partition the space with drawer dividers to keep like items together in the compartments. Make sure everything has an assigned space.

84 Bulletin board basics

A bulletin board is like a garden. If you don't attend to your garden, it will become overgrown with weeds and the flowers will be obstructed. Likewise, outdated papers on a bulletin board, if not weeded out from time to time, will obscure relevant and timely information that a bulletin board is meant to display. To keep your bulletin board alive and thriving, update the contents frequently and do a major purge every two months. To maintain a neater appearance, keep papers confined within the outer edges of the board.

QUICK TIP: **A Phone Log**

To avoid having phone messages jotted down on random scraps of paper, keep a phone log near the phone in the kitchen and train family members to write all messages in the log.

85 Turn the inside of a cabinet into a bulletin board

Fasten cork tiles with industrial-strength double-sided tape on the inside of a cabinet to create a spot where you can post important messages, schedules, invitations, and reminders. You can also post a recipe here to keep it clean while you cook. The cork should be thick enough to stick a pushpin into. For the design-minded, cover the cork with your favorite fabric by stapling or tacking the fabric to the back of the tile.

86 How to assemble a spontaneous dinner party

Take a five-step approach.

1. Keep basics in stock. These include a case of sparkling water, several bottles of red and white wine, and frozen gourmet desserts.

2. Plan an easy menu. A meal of pasta, a simple salad, and garlic bread is a no-fuss crowd pleaser.

3. Consolidate shopping. Avoid running around for wine, supplies, flowers, and specialty items. Keep most of what you need on hand and limit your shopping to fresh ingredients only.

4. Create ambiance. Nothing sets a mood like music. Create several dinner party playlists to choose from on your MP3 player or computer for different occasions and seasons.

5. Improvise table decorations. Use what's around. Instead of buying flowers, make a centerpiece by floating tea light candles in a vase of water. Garnish a fall table with multicolored leaves and acorns. Fill a bowl with lemons.

87 The basic bar setup

The following are the foundation for a well-stocked home bar:

Wine and beer. Keep a stash of your favorite white wines and beers in the refrigerator. Have a range of red wines on hand: a Malbec or Shiraz goes with meat, and have a Chianti with pasta and red sauce.

Soft drinks and mixers. Have cola and diet cola, tonic water, club soda, sparkling water, bitters, sour mix, Tabasco, lime juice, orange juice, cranberry juice, and tomato juice.

Garnishes. Lemon, lime, salt, sugar, olives, and celery round out the selection.

Liqueurs. The most popular include triple sec, Irish crème, coffee liqueur, and vermouth.

Liquors. These include vodka, gin, whiskey, rum, tequila, and brandy/cognac. Whiskey can be Scotch or American, but if you want to stock only one, choose American because most mixed whiskey drinks (like the manhattan) are made with bourbon. Whiskey can also take Coke or sour mix or simply be served on the rocks. With vodka and gin, you can make almost any drink (by adding juice, vermouth, bitters, tonic, or just ice).

88 How to store wine

Nigel Carr, former CEO of Oriel Wines, offers the following advice to ensure proper preservation of wine:

- Store wine away from direct light, which can damage or prematurely age your wine. Ultraviolet light can even penetrate dark-colored glass and impart unpleasant aromas.
- Optimum long-term storage temperature is 50 to 55°F, and sudden dramatic changes in temperature should be avoided. That said, wine will likely last for a year or two between 40 and 70°F, as long as changes in temperature are gradual rather than sudden.
- Humidity should be between 50 and 80 percent so that the cork doesn't dry out and crumble or lose its seal.
- Store wine on its side rather than upright to keep the cork damp.
- Wine should be stored in a calm place, as excessive vibration can disturb the sediment and damage the wine.
- Face the label upward so that you don't disturb the bottle to check what it is.
- Store all wine accessibly so that you're not constantly moving it to get to the bottle you want to drink.

If your most special wine will be opened in a year or two, then you certainly don't need a wine refrigerator. However, if you're saving a special case of wine from the year of your marriage or your child's birth for a big celebration a couple of decades later, then a wine refrigerator is a worthy investment. You should be able to go online and find a decent one to store two or three cases of wine for $400 to $600. Don't worry about the state of your labels, which could potentially rot even in the most antiseptic wine refrigerator. Just be sure to keep a record of what you have on each shelf in case the labels fall off the bottles.

Sanctuaries
Bedrooms and Closets

An organized bedroom is the key to cultivating a balanced, happy, and relaxed state of mind. But these days, flat-screen TVs, kids' toys, computers, and exercise machines have turned our supposed oases of serenity into all-purpose family rooms. To reclaim your sanctuary, limit bedroom activities to dressing, romancing, reading, and, of course, resting.

89 How to get the most out of bedroom furniture

Choose bedroom storage solutions that give you extra space while hiding what's inside. Here are some essentials:

• Use a dresser instead of open shelving. Unless you fold your
T-shirts like a veteran Gap employee, open shelving is best left
to the closet, where chaos can be concealed behind closed doors.
• Reduce nightstand clutter by stashing nightly essentials such as hand lotion, lip moisturizer, and reading glasses in the drawer and out of sight.
• A trunk or hollow bench at the foot of the bed can store extra pillows, blankets, and linens or out-of-season clothing, as well as provide an extra perch in the room.
• Lift-up storage beds and beds with built-in drawers are great ways to put unused space to work.
• A headboard with storage cubbies gets books and magazines off the floor and within arm's reach.

90 Five bedside table tips

What is kept on your nightstand reveals a lot about your habits. Use the following tips to edit your bedside bedlam:

1. Choose a nightstand that supports your nightly habits. If you read a lot in bed, go for a nightstand with a shelf for books. It's not essential that you and your partner have matching bedside tables if your needs are different.

2. Keep only things you use nightly, such as a reading lamp, alarm clock, phone, reading glasses, remotes (if you must), hand cream, a water pitcher and/or glass.

3. Relocate medications and vitamins to the kitchen (see entry 80, "Managing medications") and batteries to a utility closet. To encourage undisrupted sleep patterns, keep radiation-emitting cell phones and chargers away from your brain.

4. Instead of displaying trinkets, memories, and odds and ends, which all add up to clutter, choose just one special piece.

5. Use a small tray to contain items such as lip balm, reading glasses, and jewelry you take off at night, especially if your bedside table doesn't have a drawer.

91 Found space: under the bed

Feng shui experts advise storing nothing under the bed. However, if your storage needs demand it, then store out-of-season clothing and extra bedding—soft items that are comfortable to sleep on top of—rather than things that may stimulate the mind such as books and papers. Underbed storage boxes keep things clean, contained, and easier to access. Eight clear plastic underbed boxes from the Container Store fit comfortably under a full-sized bed. Gather similar things together in each box and label the outside with the label pointing toward you. Toss a few cedar blocks into each box to deter fabric-hungry pests.

92 Three essentials for a neat bedroom

1. Make the bed every morning. This not only forces you to clear the clutter off it daily but also transforms your room's appearance.

2. Keep a basket near the door for items that belong elsewhere in the house and redistribute them daily.

3. Clear surfaces (dressers, nightstands, chairs, and floor) of the day's accumulations every night. If you make it a nightly ritual, it takes only a few minutes and clutter doesn't build up.

93 Extra blankets and pillows

Store spare blankets and pillows in the zippered plastic bags they came in. If you don't still have these, try Ziploc XL and XXL plastic bags. Save space with these by squeezing (or vacuuming) the air out of the bag to compress the contents. Ziploc bags protect against dust, allergens, dirt, bugs, and moisture, so they are good for long-term storage, too. Be sure to check seals from time to time and air blankets and pillows out at least every six months. Keep blankets and pillows on a high shelf in the linen closet or in the closet of the guest bedroom if that's where they'll be used.

94 Bed linens

Keep a maximum of three sets of sheets per bed. This way, you can have one on the bed, one in the laundry, and one in the linen closet. If space is *really* tight, reduce the number to two sets—one to use and one to wash. To store sheet sets, take the flat sheet, fitted sheet, and one or more pillowcases and put them inside the other pillowcase. The result: stackable bundles that sit neatly on a shelf and are easy to grab and use when needed.

95　How to fold a fitted sheet

1. Pinch the inside seams of the corners at one end of the sheet. Bring your hands together and fit the corner in your right hand into the corner in your left hand. Lay it on the bed or on any other clean, flat surface.

2. Pick up the other two fitted corners and pinch the inside seams, again bringing your hands together to fit the corners into each other in the same way.

3. Hold one pair of corners in one hand and the other pair in the other hand and bring your hands together, tucking the corners in your right hand into the corners held by your left hand.

4. Lay the sheet down on the bed so that the fitted corners form a crescent moon at the bottom right corner. Smooth out the wrinkles, working from the center to the edges.

5. Fold up the bottom edge toward the center to hide the elastic and make a straight edge.

6. Fold the top down to the bottom to make a long rectangle.

7. Fold one side into the middle.

8. Fold again into thirds and into a neat square package.

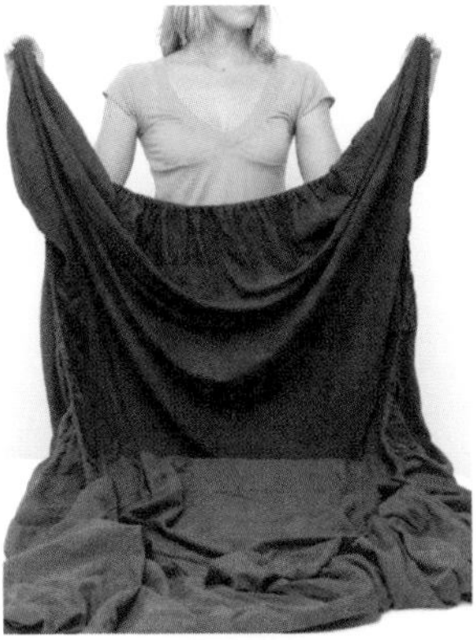
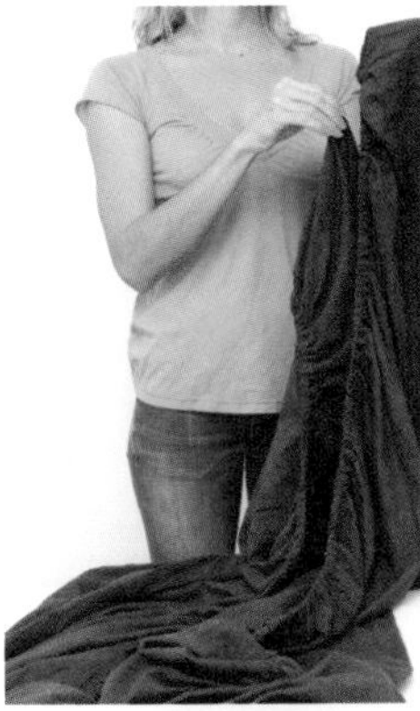
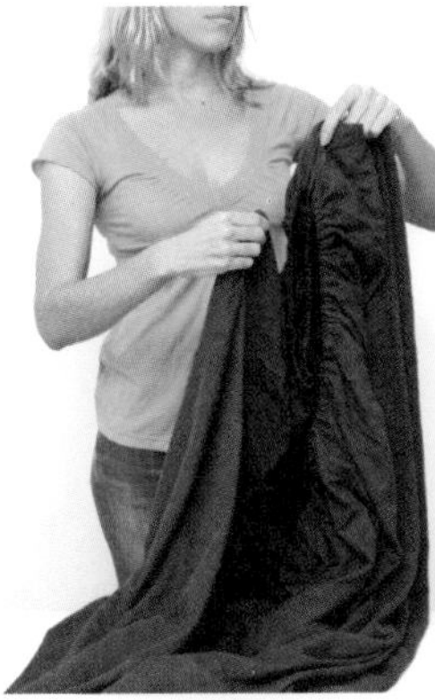
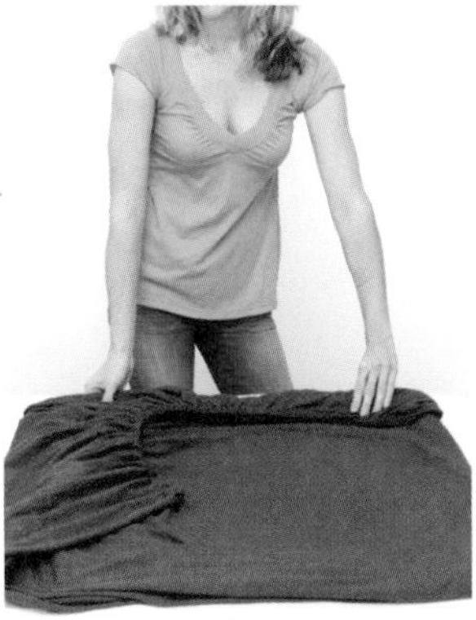
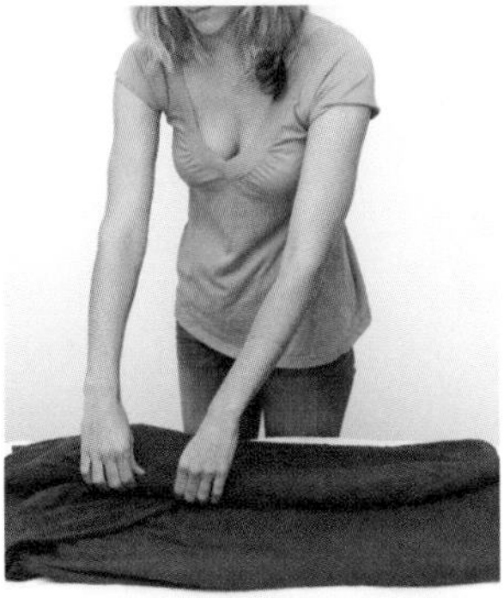
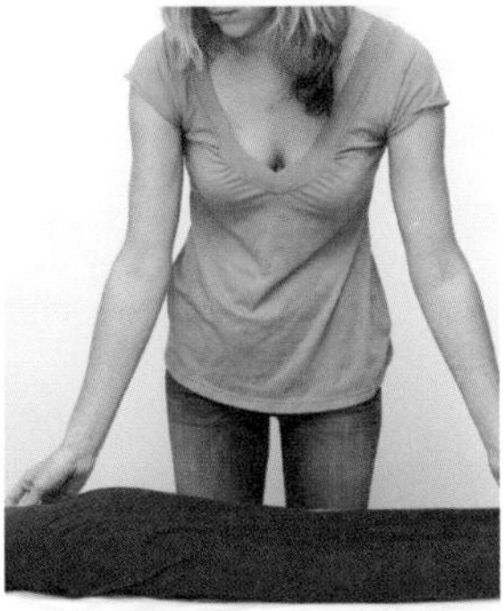
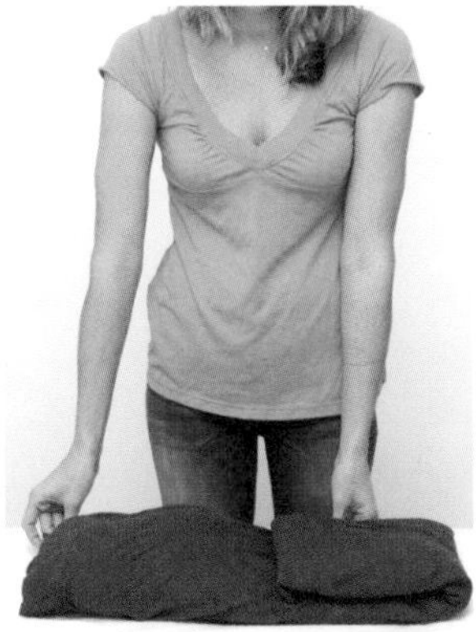
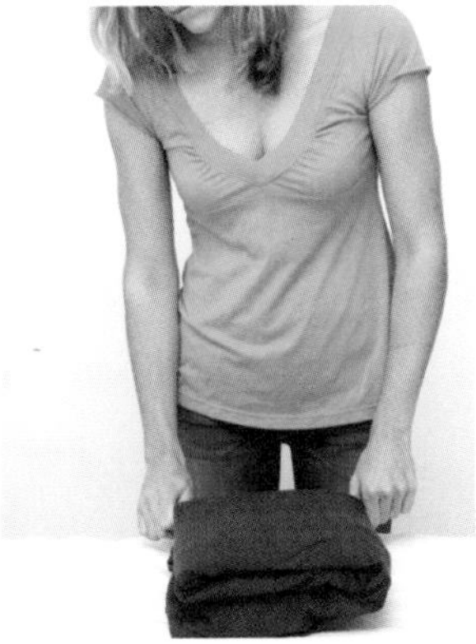

96   Organize your closet

Label four boxes (bags will also do): TOSS, DONATE, SELL, and FIX. Obviously if you don't plan to sell anything, then you won't need that box. Feel free to add a box for any other relevant category (such as stuff you'll give your sister, rather than donate). Then use the bed as a sorting area for items you plan to keep, making separate piles for shirts, pants, suits, skirts, dresses, etc.

What to donate

Anything out of style, unflattering, itchy, too small, or too big is ripe for the donation box. Donate only those items that are in good condition and wearable. If you don't have a favorite local charity, the American Red Cross has offices across the country. Donate used women's business clothing to Dress for Success, which provides professional attire to disadvantaged women and has locations worldwide. Career Gear is the men's equivalent, with affiliates in New York City, Boston, Houston, Miami, Washington, D.C., and New Haven, Connecticut. You can claim a tax deduction provided you obtain a receipt for your donation.

What to toss

Get rid of anything ripped, stretched out of shape, stained, or damaged beyond repair. Charities such as Goodwill use only about *half* of the clothing they receive. They won't accept anything torn or soiled, so save them the hassle of having to throw away the undesirables you've donated and instead recycle your armpit-stained T-shirts into rags or just throw them away.

The maybe pile

If you aren't sure you are ready to let go of something, use the "maybe" pile as a halfway house. If you still aren't sure, enlist the opinion of an honest friend. And if you still aren't sure after that, box up the items and store them away. If after six months you haven't thought of those clothes, you can safely let them go.

97 How to decide what to keep

Don't succumb to garment guilt

See if you recognize any of the following poor reasons to keep something:

1. **"I might want to wear it again someday."** If you haven't worn something in a year (unless it's black tie), then it's dead weight in your closet.

2. **"I'm going to diet back into it."** If you haven't been the size in question in more than a year, let it go. When you lose the weight, go out and treat yourself to something new.

3. **"It might come back into style."** Fashion cycles are long, and it can take over a decade for something to come back in style. And when it does, it will be updated with a slightly different look.

4. **"It was very expensive."** It's painful to let go of something you paid a lot of money for and never wore. If it is a designer piece, consign it. If not, donate it for a tax deduction, and you'll no longer be reminded of your shopping blunder.

5. **Any "if" statement such as, "I'd wear that if I ever go on a cruise to Alaska."** Unless you already have your tickets in hand, get rid of it. By the time you take that trip, if ever, I give you permission to go out and buy just the right thing.

6. **"I want to save it for my daughter."** Ladies, unless it's couture, she probably won't want it.

7. **"I feel guilty."** If your poor aunt Sally took three years to knit a sweater with her arthritic hands, but it isn't quite your style, then give Aunt Sally a hug while wearing it once, and then make sure some less-fortunate person stays just a little warmer this winter. It's a win-win.

Four great reasons to keep it
1. You love it.
2. It's flattering.
3. You feel great in it.
4. It projects the right image (whatever "right" is to you).

Most important, love everything you own. If you love everything in your closet, getting dressed is stress-free and fun.

QUICK TIP: **Recycle Old Athletic Shoes**

Nike has a program for recycling used athletic shoes (of any brand) called Reuse-A-Shoe, which repurposes materials into sport surfaces in underserved communities around the world. Drop-off locations throughout the United States can be found on the program's Web site (www.nikereuseashoe.com), or you can mail the shoes to:

Nike Recycling Center
c/o Reuse-A-Shoe
26755 SW 95th Avenue
Wilsonville, OR 97070

98   The art of consignment

Turn your clothing clutter into cash by consigning things you no longer wear. The first step is to research consignment shops in your area. (An Internet search of "consignment shops" and the name of your city will bring up a handful of options, or check www. howtoconsign.com.) Choose one that carries the kind of items you are looking to unload. Some consignment shops accept only high-end designer labels, while others specialize in kids' clothing. Ask whether they accept clothes seasonally (can you bring them a winter coat in summer?) and find out what they do with unsold merchandise (do they donate it, throw it away, or ask you to come get it?). If you have heaps of clothing, make sure they don't have a limit on how much one person can consign. Consigners vary in what and how they pay. Ask what the split is, remembering that sometimes there's room for negotiation.

99   How to sell clothes online

EBay is a great venue for selling nationally recognizable brands. It is fairly simple to sell on eBay, but it can be time-consuming. You will be responsible for setting up an account (if you don't already have one), photographing your items, writing detailed and accurate descriptions, posting the listings, responding to questions during the auction, as well as handling payment, packaging, shipping, insurance, and returns. If you would like to sell on eBay but don't have the time, you can hire a Trading Assistant, an experienced eBay seller willing to take items on consignment and sell them for you for a fee (sometimes as high as 50 percent of the final selling price). You can find a trading assistant near you at www.ebaytradingassistant.com. Another option for selling clothing online is Craigslist (www.craigslist.com). Listings are free, and since it's local, you can save the cost and hassle of shipping by arranging for pickup. Frequent Craigslist sellers recommend selling in lots rather than one piece at a time.

QUICK TIP: **Closet Rotation**

To figure out which clothes you actually wear, try this experiment: Rehang clothes on the rod with the opening of the hanger hook facing toward you. When you wear an item, turn the hanger around the right way. At the end of a season, you'll easily see that any hangers with the hook still backward on the rod hold clothes you haven't worn. Consider getting rid of them.

bedrooms and closets

100 Closet design savvy

When designing or reconfiguring a closet, follow these tips:

1. **Sort your wardrobe.** Group each type of clothing (jackets, shirts, skirts, pants, and dresses) and hang them together on a rod or rack. Measure how much space is required for each category.

2. **Maximize space.** Install rods where they are most useful. Position rods eleven to twelve inches from the back wall, allowing items twenty-two to twenty-four inches of depth and thirty-two to thirty-six inches of vertical hanging space.

3. **Install drawers.** Small items like socks and scarves are best stored in drawers. Bear in mind, however, that drawers are the most expensive component of a closet. If you have a dresser elsewhere in the room, consider limiting or eliminating closet drawer space.

4. **Build in cubbies.** Cubes are a see-at-a-glance solution for storing such items as sweaters, purses, hats, jeans, and shoes.

5. **Accessorize your closet.** Add bells and whistles such as specialized racks for belts, ties, shoes, and bags, which keep these smaller items from becoming a jumble.

6. **Use every inch.** Claim air rights by adding shelves above racks for extra storage. Hooks on closet doors afford quick access to frequently used items like tote bags.

The nuts and bolts: Clothing can weigh a lot. To avoid collapse, make sure to select the correct anchors when attaching rods and shelves. For Sheetrock walls, the anchor should be attached to the studs. For lath and plaster walls, use molly bolts, which have spring winged tips that expand once inserted into the wall and distribute weight better than a regular screw bolt. For plaster and brick walls, use lead or plastic shields.

101 Hanging versus folding

To maximize space, hang as much as your closet allows. Also, most clothing will retain its shape and appearance better when hung. Dresses, suits, pressed shirts, blouses, dress pants, skirts, and delicate fabrics (silk, velvet, chiffon) or those prone to wrinkling (cotton, linen, rayon) should definitely be hung. Never hang sweaters or knits, which will stretch. For the same reason, fold anything heavily beaded or ornamented. T-shirts, sweats, and workout clothing should be folded on shelves or in cubbies or drawers, and organize socks and lingerie in a drawer. Casual-wear pants like jeans, khakis, or corduroys can be either folded or hung.

102 Hanger handbook

1. This classic style hanger for hanging tops and jackets has notches to ensure that dresses or tops with thin straps won't slip.

2. This multifunctional suit hanger works with tops and jackets, and the bar makes it perfect for women's suits and coordinates.

3. The extra-wide shoulders of this suit hanger are best for maintaining the contour of men's suits and coats.

4. This combination hanger is an alternate to the suit hanger with a bar. Hang skirts by the waistband and pants by the cuffs, folded on the crease. Clips should be padded to protect clothing.

5. This hanger works for all types of pants and skirts, especially dressy fabrics that might crease if hung over a bar. Moveable clips accommodate various sized waistbands or pant-leg widths.

6. A padded hanger is a must for delicate materials. Some come with chrome studs on the shoulders to prevent thin straps from slipping.

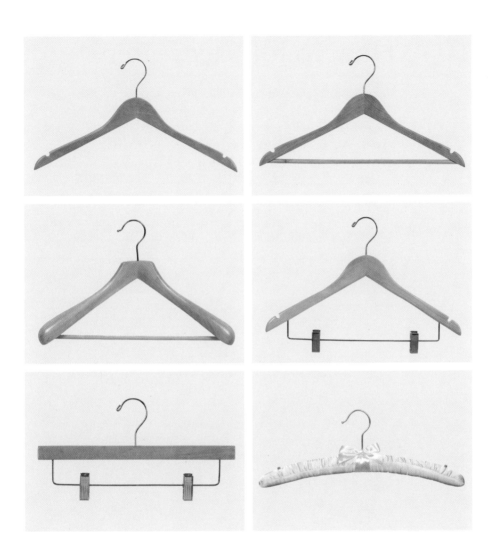

103 How to fold a sweater

1. Lay a sweater facedown on a flat surface with the bottom edge closest to you. Fold one sleeve straight across the back toward the opposite shoulder without bringing the side in. Do the same with the other sleeve, resting it on top of the first.

2. Fold one side in halfway (shoulder should be in the middle of the sweater) and then fold the other side in to meet it.

3. Bring the bottom of the sweater halfway up, and then up again, making two folds (if it is long) or all the way up to the neckline (for short or bulky sweaters).

4. Flip it over.

104 How to fold a T-shirt

1. Lay the T-shirt facedown on a flat surface with its bottom edge closest to you and smooth it out.

2. Fold the left side in vertically so that the shoulder edge comes to the middle of the neckline (or to the desired width). Fold the sleeve back. Repeat on other side.

3. Bring the bottom of the T-shirt up to fold it in half.

4. Flip it over.

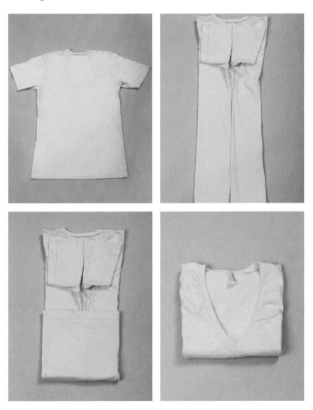

105   How to store delicates

Delicate fabrics such as linen, silk, taffeta, and chiffon, as well as beaded or otherwise ornamented garments, require special care. If possible, roll delicates instead of folding them in order to avoid creasing and stretching. Pad folded garments with acid-free storage tissue paper and refold them occasionally to avoid deterioration of the fabric along the crease. These items should be stored in a well-ventilated spot away from direct light where they won't be disturbed. Never store delicate garments in vinyl or plastic.

106   How to avoid moth damage

Insects are most attracted to animal fibers such as wool, cashmere, silk, down, leather, and mohair as well as other natural fibers such as linen and cotton. But they will also dine on synthetics stained with food, drink, sweat, or blood, so make sure clothing is put away clean. Mothballs not only smell bad, they also contain toxic chemicals. Cedar and lavender are natural pest repellents and work well when stored with clothing in an airtight container. (See entry 20, "Three ways to avoid mothballs and mildew.") If critters have eaten holes in your clothing, dry-clean or wash items in hot water to kill pests and their eggs. Or put the affected piece and others nearby in a plastic bag and freeze for seventy-two hours, as moths and their larvae cannot survive frigid temperatures. Always clean the storage area thoroughly before putting clothes back.

107   Divide and conquer shelves

Shelf dividers can help in managing stacks of sweaters or heaps of handbags. They slip easily over the front edge of any solid shelf and can be positioned as close together or as far apart as you need. The effect is a cubbylike enclosure for stacks of sweaters, T-shirts, or purses. Shelf dividers come in a variety of styles and materials, such as acrylic or wire.

108   Why to dump dry-cleaning plastic

When clothing comes back from the dry cleaner, remove the plastic and rehang the item on a proper hanger. Wire hangers are a closet's worst enemy. They damage clothing by creating bumps in the shoulder, and they tangle easily on the rod by leaving no space between hanging clothes. If there is any air moisture in the air, plastic bags will trap it against the clothing fibers, causing mold and mildew to grow. Natural fibers such as wool, silk, cotton, and linen can't breathe when trapped in plastic. Furthermore, dry-cleaning chemicals may discolor clothes or cause them to fade if kept in plastic too long. To protect clothing that you don't wear often from dust or daylight, use a fabric garment bag instead.

109 Winter and summer: rotate your closet

Editing your closet seasonally is a great way to regularly cull your wardrobe. This is the time to take a look at what you didn't wear and figure out what items you are missing. Take advantage of end-of-season sales to fill in any gaps in your wardrobe. When storing out-of-season clothing, remember to clean it before you pack it away. As mentioned earlier (see entry 106, "How to avoid moth damage"), pests are attracted to clothing stained with food, drink, and/or sweat. Also make sure that clothing is completely dry before it is stored. Any moisture will creaate a mildew- and mold-friendly environment. In humid climates, add a silica gel packet to absorb moisture. Fold clothes with white acid-free tissue storage paper to prevent wrinkling and store in airtight plastic storage containers with cedar or lavender sachets. Label boxes and store them under the bed or on a high shelf in the closet. Don't pack clothes in too tightly—allow them room to breathe.

110 Jewels and baubles

If you can, dedicate a narrow top drawer to jewelry. With jewelry tray inserts, subdivide the drawer to contain and separate pieces of jewelry so that they don't tangle and you can see what you have at a glance. Or simply use the cardboard boxes the jewelry came in, putting the lid underneath the box and positioning them side by side to make your own drawer dividers. Store silver in a felt or velvet pouch to delay tarnishing, and store pearls by themselves in a cotton or silk pouch to prevent scratching.

111 No more tangles

The best way to keep necklaces untangled is to hang them. If you want to display them on top of a dresser, use something they can dangle from, such as a ceramic hand or bust. Or repurpose a countertop hand towel stand to hold chunkier necklaces. To save surface space, mount a set of hooks on a wall or on the inside of a closet door. Peel-and-stick hooks will support daintier necklaces.

QUICK TIP: **Chain Keeper**

If storing necklaces in a drawer, cut a slit in a strip of cardboard toward the top left and the bottom right sides. Wrap a single necklace around the cardboard to protect it from tangling and tuck ends into the slits. Store in a felt bag for additional protection.

112 Tiny things: earrings

The key to organizing earrings is to group them by pairs so that one doesn't go missing and they don't get jumbled up. You should always be able to locate both at once, and not have to turn a box or drawer upside down to find a missing mate. Use small porcelain dishes to store individual pairs.

bedrooms and closets

TRAVEL CONTAINERS

When traveling, store jewelry in clear stackable screw-on vitamin containers. Screw together as many compartments as you need for a trip and toss them in your suitcase.

113 Where to empty your pockets

Designate a container on a flat surface in your closet or bedroom for what comes out of your pockets. Assign categories for your daily discharge and contain accordingly. Place a small tray on a dresser or shelf for personal effects such as cell phone, wallet, and sunglasses. Add a bowl or jar to collect small change and a box with a lid for receipts or business cards. (When receipts pile up, see entry 170, "Saving receipts.") When change fills your container, take it to a local supermarket or bank and claim your cash.

QUICK TIP: **Spare Buttons**

Designate a box for spare buttons and keep a fine-point indelible ink pen inside. When you buy a new item of clothing with a spare button, which usually comes in a small plastic or paper bag, write a brief description of the garment on the bag (to identify it when you need it) and put it in the box. When the box gets full, throw out buttons for clothing you no longer own.

114 Purse patrol

If you have trouble locating your purses and totes, try a handbag organizer, which makes viewing and then choosing a bag easy. For a clutter-free bedroom, keep the back of your bedroom door clear and mount hooks on the inside of a closet door instead. If you can allot space on the shelf above the rod, store handbags there, but use shelf dividers so that purses remain upright. To protect vintage or other precious bags, clear plastic handbag boxes are a good solution in terms of stackability and visibility. Keep handbags in the dust bags that they came with to protect them from light and dirt. Stuff them with tissue paper or bubble wrap so they maintain their shape. (Avoid newspaper, which leaves print marks on lighter-colored linings.) Organize bags by style and color to make for quicker selection.

115 How to fold silk scarves

To store delicate silk scarves, lay them on the bed (or a flat surface) one at a time. Fold each scarf in half and then in half again, making a square (or fold according to the creases), and then wrap it in white acid-free tissue paper. The tissue paper will keep scarves from wrinkling. Stack them on top of one another in a shallow drawer rather than on a shelf. Take care to put them away properly between wearings. Makers of fine silk scarves, such as Hermès, recommend storing scarves in the boxes in which they came.

bedrooms and closets

116 Wardrobe essentials for women…

Make sure to invest in at least one top-quality garment in each of the following categories:

1. Basic black dress
2. Day dress
3. A-line skirt
4. Tailored dress pants
5. Nice jeans
6. White dress shirt
7. Cashmere sweater
8. Blazer
9. Trench coat
10. Classic handbag

...and for men

1. Black or other dark-colored suit
2. Topcoat
3. Blazer
4. Cashmere sweater
5. White or blue button-down shirt
6. Dress pants
7. Nice jeans in a dark wash
8. Khakis
9. Tie
10. Pair of oxfords, and a belt to match

117 Three ways to organize shoes

Gather all your shoes into one sorting area. First weed out the ones you don't want. Then group the keepers into categories such as athletic, casual, work, and evening. Depending on the space and setup of your closet, there are three options:

1. **Boxes.** If you have the space, the least expensive solution is to keep shoes in their original box, and either tape a photo to the outside of the box or simply write a description on a label with a bold pen. This works best for shoes you don't wear that often but want to keep clean and protected. Clear acrylic stacking shoe boxes provide a cleaner, more uniform appearance.

2. **Racks.** An over-the-door version keeps shoes off the floor, saves space, and makes it easy to get to what you want. That said, one of the most *ineffective* organizing solutions is a shoe rack on a closet floor. Who wants to bend down and wade through hanging clothes to return a pair of shoes to a rack on the floor?

3. **Shelves and cubbies.** This is my favorite method. Cubbies are the most space-efficient way to keep pairs of shoes together and accessible. Shelves are best for displaying shoes so that they can be seen easily. To make use of dead space corners in a reach-in closet, try a modular shoe cubby, which can be customized to fit in tight spaces.

QUICK TIP: **Shoe Rehab**

Before you throw out those well-worn shoes you loved, literally, to death, consider sending them to rehab. A good shoemaker can seal cracks and splits in leather and rubber soles, fix or obscure deep scratches in the shoe's upper, and even tend to mechanical problems such as rebuilding heels and mending leaks, and hence working miracles with shoes you thought were on their last leg.

what's a disorganized person to do?

black suede pumps

118 Sock drawer first aid

Dump your sock collection on the bed. Match pairs, throw away socks with holes, and set aside single socks. (See 201, "New uses for old socks.") Take the remaining pairs and separate them by type: sport socks, dress socks, panty hose. Measure your sock drawer and figure out which type of organizer will accommodate your collection. Drawer dividers allow you to keep sock types together, whereas a waffle-style organizer separates individual pairs. Rolling socks and folding one over to make a ball is a good way to keep athletic socks together, but doing so can stretch out the elastic in socks made out of natural fibers like wool or cashmere.

QUICK TIP: **Color-blind**

If you have trouble differentiating between black, brown, and blue socks, try this method. Use spring-loaded drawer organizers to separate any drawer into three compartments, one for each color. Label the sections along the top edge

of the front of the drawer BLUE, BROWN, and BLACK, and never again be surprised in the sunlight that your socks don't match your suit.

119 Ties and belts

Store ties and belts so you can see them at a glance. If rod space is your only option, opt for a tie or belt hanger that rotates, giving access to all ties or belts. (Traditional tie hangers make it hard to see what's on the far side.) For extensive tie collections, tie hangers can be mounted on the rod and operated with the press of a button. Another option, if space permits, is tie and belt racks that hang from a closet wall or door. These enable you to see all the belts or ties at once.

120 How to organize underwear

First things first. Mind mother's warning and immediately discard anything you wouldn't want to be caught wearing should you be hit by a truck. Think overstretched elastic, rips, holes, and stains. Also eliminate underthings that don't fit or are uncomfortable. Rather than trying to fold underwear into neat piles, use drawer dividers to separate panties by style (briefs, thongs, bikinis, boy shorts, etc.), so that when you are looking for a particular style to suit a certain pair of pants, you can narrow your selection by having each kind grouped together.

121 Bras and lingerie

Like panties, organize lingerie into categories. If possible, keep bras and underwear in separate drawers. Use narrow drawer dividers to separate bras by color—black, nude/white, and other colors. Choose larger boxes for other lingerie, separating slips from camisoles and other pieces. Choose dividers made from plastic or that are covered with fabric (silk, canvas, linen), as wood can snag delicates. Measure drawers before shopping for drawer inserts, or look for customizable ones.

122 To the cleaners

Keep a separate laundry basket for items that need dry cleaning. Look for hampers with removable cloth bags for transporting clothes to the cleaners. Place wire hangers here too, so that they can be returned to the cleaners on your next trip. A divided hamper can also be used to keep dry cleaning separate from dirty laundry.

123 Get more closet space without renovating

First look for unused space. Is there dead space above the top shelf? If so, put in a second shelf there. Is there room to install another rod? Are the backs of the closet doors being put to use? Install racks or hooks to create space for ties, belts, shoes, or a bathrobe. Is there an awkward nook that isn't being used? Add something that gives access to the space such as a set of pull-out drawers. Sometimes it also helps to think *outside* the closet. An armoire or a wardrobe can provide extra hanging space or be configured to provide auxiliary storage for shoes, handbags, sweaters, and other accessories.

124 Keeping your closet tidy

1. Make a habit of putting things back where they belong.
   If clothing is arranged by type (shirts, pants, skirts, suits, etc.),
   with matching hangers, and there's plenty of space between
   items in the closet, it should then be easy and even enjoyable
   to put things away in the right place.

2. Take care when putting things back. Take the time to fold or hang
   clothes properly rather than just shoving them into the closet.

3. Remove plastic and wire hangers from dry cleaning and rehang
   items on their designated hangers.

4. When something new comes in, something old should go.

5. Go through your closet at least two times per year (at the change
   of seasons) to purge what you no longer wear.

Life's Necessities
Bathrooms

Products, potions, pills, and lotions:
The modern bathroom is utilitarian,
to be sure, but it has evolved to be
much more than that. Organize it
right and even the busiest bathroom
can be a retreat and haven. Morning
and evening rituals performed in a
clutter-free environment will have
a calming effect—the best way to
start and end your day.

125 Bathroom first aid

Organize your bathroom in three easy steps:

1. Sort. You can tackle the whole bathroom at once or break it down into smaller projects by choosing specific areas, such as the medicine cabinet. Set up a sorting area. Get three boxes and a garbage bag.
   - Box one: Items you use every day
   - Box two: Things you use regularly
   - Box three: Items that belong elsewhere (including things to be donated)
   - Garbage bag: Half-empty shampoo bottles, anything dusty (a good sign you haven't used it in a while), anything rusty (think old scissors, razors, tweezers), old toothbrushes (replace yours every three months), and expired medications, cosmetics, and products

(See entries 128 and 129, "How to safely dispose of medications," and "When to toss: cosmetics.")

2. Store. The products and items you use every day, such as your toothbrush, should be the easiest to access. Put these in the medicine cabinet, top drawer, or place them (sparingly) on the counter. The things you use regularly but not daily can be stored under the sink, in lower drawers, or in a stand-alone cabinet, étagère, or shelves. (See entry 127, "One-Hour Project: The medicine cabinet.")

3. Contain. Keep bathroom items contained according to their purpose. Assemble activity baskets for hair care, nail care, first aid, pet grooming supplies, and travel. Keep brushes, combs, gel, mousse, and blow dryer together in a basket under the sink. Store nail polish, remover, and manicure tools in an acrylic box in the medicine cabinet. Pack all your first aid remedies into a clear zippered bag or plastic box and store it under the sink.

126 Medicine cabinet: remedies

- **Divide shelves.** Place acrylic drawer organizers on medicine cabinet shelves to keep like items, such as nail care supplies, together. Acrylic risers provide extra surface space and put unused vertical space between shelves to work.
- **Improvise containers.** Look to the kitchen or other rooms for creative ones. A wide ceramic mug or canning jar can serve as a container for cotton balls, while a creamer can hold cotton swabs.
- **Find hidden space.** Hang a magnetic strip on the inside of the medicine cabinet door (between shelves), and hang metal objects such as tweezers, nail clippers, and spare shaving blades. Magnetic strips with adhesive back are available at hardware stores.
- **Use hooks.** Add magnetized hooks to hold ponytail holders or scissors. A magnetic notepad holder (usually found on a fridge) can hold brushes and combs or toothbrushes and toothpaste.

127 One-Hour Project
The medicine cabinet

Chances are you can complete this project in under an hour.

1. Take everything out and wipe medicine cabinet shelves clean.

2. Discard expired medications and products (see entries 128 and 129, "How to safely dispose of medications" and "When to toss: cosmetics") as well as anything else you no longer use.

3. Relocate medications to a cool, dry place such as the kitchen. (See entry 80, "Managing medications.")

4. Group items together according to what they are used for—hair care and styling, skin and body care, makeup, and so on.

5. Assign shelves for the various categories, keeping products used most often on easy-to-access shelves.

6. If bottles don't fit on shelves, decant them into smaller bottles with labels and store the bigger ones under the sink.

7. Keep similar items contained together, especially if they are small. (See entry 126, "Medicine cabinet: remedies," for specific ideas.)

128 How to safely dispose of medications

It is generally *not* safe to flush medications down the toilet or drain. Chemicals in these medications are being found in excessive quantities in streams, rivers, and lakes. The federal National Drug Control Policy advises to:

• Take unused, unneeded, or expired prescription drugs out of their original containers.
• Mix medications to be discarded with used coffee grounds or kitty litter, and put them in impermeable containers such as empty cans or sealable bags. This will ensure that the drugs are not diverted or accidentally ingested by children or pets.
• Throw these containers in the trash.
• Flush prescription drugs down the toilet only if the accompanying patient information specifically instructs that it is safe to do so.
• Return unused, unneeded, or expired prescription drugs to pharmaceutical take-back locations, which allow the public to bring unused drugs to a central location for safe disposal. Check with your local pharmacy or contact community-based household hazardous waste collection programs. Visit www.smarxtdisposal.net for more information.

QUICK TIP: **Expiry Dates**

Most medications expire one to three years from the time of manufacture. Some medications merely lose their effectiveness over time, but others actually degrade and become toxic. If an open bottle of aspirin, for instance, has a vinegary smell, that's a sign that it has begun to degrade. When in doubt, throw it out.

129 When to toss: cosmetics

Once exposed to air, cosmetics start to lose effectiveness and the ability to combat bacteria. The chart below offers a general guideline, but celebrated makeup artist Pati Dubroff notes that some products (with the exception of mascara) can last longer than indicated if stored in a cool place away from sunlight. Lipsticks, foundations, and other cream-based formulas are more subject to spoilage than powders. She advises discarding a product if there is a change in smell or it has been exposed to heat.

Product	Shelf Life
LIQUID AND CREAM FOUNDATION	6-12 months
CONCEALER	8-12 months
PRESSED POWDER*	1 year
EYE SHADOW	1 year
BLUSH	1 year
MASCARA	3 months
LIPSTICK AND LIP GLOSS	2 years
EYE AND LIP PENCILS	2 years
FACIAL CLEANSER	1 year
FACIAL TONER	1 year
FACIAL MOISTURIZER	1 year

Pressed powder spoils faster if stored with puffs, which tend to accumulate oil. If kept separately from puffs and sponges, these powders can last up to three years.

130 No-muss makeup

Incorporate dividers into a bathroom drawer to separate compacts, eye shadows, lipsticks, eye pencils, and mascara. Then you can see everything at a glance. If it is hard to tell blush or eye shadow compacts apart, store them upside down so that you can read the color on the label. If you don't have drawer space, you can opt for a divided makeup bag that can be stored underneath the bathroom sink.

131 Combat counter clutter

We all want easy access to the things we use daily, but that doesn't mean everything has to be in plain sight. In the bathroom below, products were strewn around the sink. My client identified the eight items that she uses daily (including toothpaste, dental floss, facial cleanser, and moisturizer), which we gathered together in a small acrylic drawer divider. Cotton swabs, mud mask, and body lotion went into the medicine cabinet, and styling gel went into a basket with other hair care products under the sink.

132 One-Hour Project
Bathroom vanity

1. Take everything out of the cabinet and throw out or donate what you don't use. (See entry 125, "Bathroom first aid.")

2. Clean inside the cabinet with some soapy water or nontoxic all-purpose cleaner.

3. Group products together into categories that make sense, creating "activity" baskets: cleaning supplies, hair care, feminine hygiene, first aid, etc.

4. Assess your empty cabinet space. Measure the depth, width, and height, noting distances from the cabinet edges to the pipes.

5. Buy containers to divide the space and accommodate whatever you need to store. Use a removable caddy or tote for cleaning supplies. Take advantage of often-overlooked vertical space with stackable plastic drawers or use a wire shelf, which will double surface space.

6. Leave a little space in each container for new purchases. You always want some room for expansion.

133   Hair it is

There are three categories of hair care items: tools (blow dryer, curling iron, straightening iron, brushes, combs, curlers), styling products (gel, mousse, spray), and accessories (barrettes, bobby pins, ponytail holders). Dedicate a deep drawer (if you have one) for the tools. Wrap cords around curling irons and blow dryers. Keep brushes, combs, and curlers together in a plastic bag (try a zippered clear vinyl sweater bag) to keep stray hairs from migrating to bathroom floors. No drawers? Stash a basket under the sink, or look for a mountable organizer for the inside of a cabinet door. For small items, try a shower curtain ring or carabiner (used for rock climbing) to keep ponytail holders together. Attach barrettes and clips to a wide piece of ribbon. Keep bobby pins in a small box with a lid.

134 Spa trick: rolled towels

Rolled towels take up less space than folded ones, and a pyramid of fresh towels make you feel like you're at the spa. Fold towels in half lengthwise and then roll them up. Determine where you have extra space in the bathroom and store towels accordingly. Rolled towels can be stored in a basket on the floor or in a pyramid on a shelf. Repurpose a window box, which takes up very little space and, depending on the size, can store rolled bath towels or hand towels.

135 Shower power

If you can't see the rim of your tub for all the bath products, try these tips:

- Think vertically. A kitchen organizer rail system is a great way to use wall space in the shower or around the tub. Stainless steel rails are fitted with different-size baskets hung by S hooks to create customizable storage. It's easy enough to make your own version with towel racks, chrome baskets, and S hooks.
- Buy smaller sizes. Ounce for ounce, you'll pay more but will probably end up saving money because of less waste. With smaller bottles, you are more likely to use up the product.
- Combine half-used bottles. Pour remnants into a single container and recycle the empties.
- Install a dispenser. Choose one with three compartments allowing for shampoo, conditioner, and shower gel. Many on the market will mount to any bathroom surface without tools.

136 Fun in the tub

Choose a mildew-resistant toy organizer, such as a mesh bag that suctions to the wall, which allows drainage. A sliding bathtub caddy cannot only hold toys but also let them drip-dry into the tub and give kids a surface on which to play.

Every few weeks, check toys for mildew and discard those that don't come clean. If possible, regularly run plastic toys through the dishwasher to sanitize.

137 Where to hang clothes to dry

Hang a tension curtain rod, the kind that uses spring tension to stay in place, high above the tub. Hang plastic hangers from the rod and, *voilà!* A hanging place for clothing to drip-dry into the tub. Multihook hangers and clothespin trees can exponentially expand the space.

138 Make bathroom cleaning easier

- Pull the shower curtain closed after use. A bunched-up curtain traps moisture in the plastic. Pulling the curtain closed allows the water to dry before mold and mildew can grow.
- Keep a squeegee on a suction hook in the shower to wipe the shower door off after each use to prevent spots and buildup.
- Keep the bathroom as dry as possible. Open a window when showering in the summer, and open the bathroom door after showering in the winter.

139 How to organize towels

Sort towels by size or type (hand, bath, washcloth, beach). Use linen organizers or shelf dividers to keep towels in neat stacks. Choose a different color towel for each bathroom or go with white all around to keep things simple. If your linen closet is small, consider storing towels in the bathroom where they are used. (See entry 134, "Spa trick: rolled towels.") Keep a maximum of three sets of towels (a bath towel, hand towel, and washcloth) per person, including guests.

140 How to fold a towel

This method saves space and helps spread out bulk so that towels appear fluffy and stack neatly on a shelf without toppling.

1. Fold the towel in half, bringing the bottom of the towel up to the top. Line up the edges and smooth it out, working from the center outward.

2. Fold in half again to form a rectangle.

3. Fold the rectangle in thirds, bringing one side into the center and then fold that side over to the other edge.

4. Stack on a shelf with the folded edge forward.

141 Four hidden spaces

1. A vertical tub-to-ceiling spring tension shower caddy will provide four or more levels of shelf space for products. Assign one to each person who shares the bathroom.

2. An over-the-toilet étagère creates instant extra storage space and can fit in almost all bathroom situations. (But be sure to leave enough space above the toilet to remove the tank lid.) Wall-mounted shelves and cubbies will do the trick, too.

3. Hang hooks, racks, or towel bars on the back of the bathroom door. An over-the-door coatrack instantly multiplies hanging space.

4. If you have the floor space, add a standing cabinet to create additional surface and storage space. Wood crates stacked on their sides or galvanized metal cubes can serve the same purpose.

142 First aid essentials

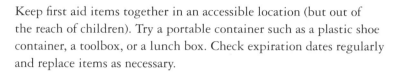

Keep first aid items together in an accessible location (but out of the reach of children). Try a portable container such as a plastic shoe container, a toolbox, or a lunch box. Check expiration dates regularly and replace items as necessary.

1. Elastic bandage

2. Adhesive bandages in a variety of sizes

3. Tweezers (a second pair, not the one you use regularly)

4. Bandage scissors (angled to cut fabric, not the wound)

5. Roll of adhesive tape

6. Sterile gauze pads

7. Triple antibiotic ointment

8. Alcohol prep pads

9. Cotton balls and swabs

10. Nonlatex exam gloves (nonallergenic and more comfy than latex gloves)

11. Oral thermometer

12. Aspirin (one aspirin during a heart attack can reduce death rates by around 25 percent) and acetaminophen, ibuprofen, or naproxen sodium to reduce pain and/or swelling

13. Hydrogen peroxide

14. First aid handbook (including phone numbers for poison control, doctors, and other emergency contacts)

143 Kitty litter solutions

If you hate the sight and smell of kitty litter, repurpose the cabinet under a bathroom sink to house the litter box and contain accompanying odors. One of my clients had a kitty-sized hole cut in the side of the cabinet and fitted it with an acrylic flap her cat could easily get through. It allowed light to enter while keeping odors in. A piece of fake turf under the litter box swept paws clean of debris. We hung the scooper from a wall hook inside the cabinet. My client just opened the cabinet doors to clean the litter box.

KITTY CABINET

A litter cabinet is a piece of furniture designed to hide a litter box. One with airtight construction traps odors inside, so you can put the litter box in any room you want. The design usually provides useful surface space on top, and some come with a drawer in which to stow kitty treats, toys, medications, and grooming tools.

The Social Hub
Living Rooms and Dens

As a shared space where everyone congregates, the family room can be a mess magnet. Toys pile up, newspapers and magazines blanket the coffee table, towers of CDs and DVDs totter, and remotes get sucked into the couch. Having proper and adequate storage—in other words, a place for everything—is key in this multifunctional room.

144 Not-so-compact disks

Plastic jewel cases for DVDs and CDs hog space. If you are attached to these cases *and* have tons of shelf space (preferably behind a closed cabinet door to avoid visual clutter), fine, but true liberation will come in the form of storage binders. These organizers let you store nearly a thousand CDs in just seventeen inches of shelf space; keep them in jewel cases and you'll fit only forty-five discs in the same amount of space. Some tips:

- Opt for binders. Ones with three metal rings allow you to rearrange CDs and DVDs when you add new ones.
- Choose a binder with a strong handle to bear the load well, a zipper closure to keep out dust, and soft insert sleeves to prevent scratching.
- Place the title or liner notes inside the sleeve with the corresponding CD or DVD on top of it. (If you loan out a disc, stick a note inside the slot with the person's name on it.)
- Label the outside of binders to easily identify their contents.
- CD binders hold more discs than DVD binders because movie title notes are larger than music ones. If you are willing to trim your movie title notes to fit them in the CD binder slots, you can store six to seven times more DVDs than if you used a proper DVD binder. Label the outside of the binders according to genre (DRAMA, COMEDY, THRILLER, DOCUMENTARY, etc.) or alphabetically (MOVIES A–L and MOVIES M–Z, for example).

QUICK TIP: **Virtual Music**

Cut CD clutter completely and go digital. There are enough home audio systems on the market that allow you to stream downloaded music from your computer to a sound system. But remember, *always* back up your music collection on an external hard drive.

what's a disorganized person to do?

145 The digital future

Just as vinyl, cassette tapes, and eight-tracks have become things of the past, so too will CDs. People are already moving toward digital music libraries, and soon—if increased broadband capabilities become more ubiquitous—even ownership of a digital library may become unnecessary. Music-on-demand is gaining popularity because people are no longer limited to their personal collections and instead can gain access to multimillion-song libraries. For a monthly fee, a number of membership-based online digital music services offer access to millions of songs that can be streamed through a computer, downloaded to a portable MP3 player, and played through a home audio system. Many let you drag and drop songs to create, edit, and share playlists without paying per track. And just as putting DVDs in binders saves shelf space, ordering movies-on-demand saves hard-drive space. Have your movies delivered digitally and instantly from a video-on-demand provider.

146   Remote possibilities

Have you ever spent twenty minutes looking for the right remote
when you could have just walked three feet to turn on the TV?
Advanced technology makes it hard to navigate the now vast world
of television without not *one,* but often *several* remotes. This means
not only more gadgets to keep track of but also more clutter on the
coffee table. Both problems can be solved with a universal remote,
which can be programmed to control TVs, DVRs, audio, and other
home entertainment systems, the least expensive of which can
control up to seven audio/visual components. Before investing in a
universal remote, be sure to check the manufacturer's compatibility
list to make sure that all your equipment will work with it. If you'd
rather stick with an army of remotes, label each of them according to
what device they operate and keep a box or tray on the coffee table to
house them.

147   How to organize books

There are several ways to sort books. As long as *you* can locate the
book you want, your system is working. Some of the most popular
methods include organizing by:

- **Genre.** Examples include:
  - Fiction
  - Nonfiction
  - Poetry
  - Art and photography
  - Cookbooks (further classified by cuisine)
  - Children's books (sorted by age level)
  - Travel guides (arranged alphabetically or by region)

- **Subject.** Organizing books by subject is good for reference books on a variety of different topics. Subjects can relate to career or hobbies. Examples of subjects might be architecture, Judaica, or politics.
- **Author.** A good option for organizing fiction and literature.
- **Size.** Books look neater when arranged by size, and you can make this system functional, too. Sometimes size corresponds to the type of book. For instance, paperback novels are short, hardcover fiction and nonfiction taller, and design books tallest. When there is a range of size within a category, group them together with the tallest in the center and shorter ones on either side.
- **Color.** If you value form over function, this is a fun way to go. While not terribly efficient for finding the book you want, organizing by color can be very visually appealing. One way to do this is to remove hardcover dust jackets. The actual spine of a hardcover book is usually a solid color. Just be aware that a jacketless book decreases in value as a collectible.

148 Seven tips for a visually organized bookshelf

1. Invest in quality bookshelves, especially if current ones are sagging.

2. Pull spines forward to the same line (a few centimeters away from the front edge of the shelf).

3. Avoid "decorating" the bookshelves with lots of little knickknacks. They will look cluttered.

4. Keep the heaviest books on the bottom shelf and other heavy ones on nonadjustable shelves. Heavy books are safer close to the ground, and having them there creates a more balanced look.

5. Adjust shelves to accommodate the height of the books. Bookshelves look better without too much "headroom" above books. Conversely, don't stack books (or anything else) on top of a row of books, as this makes a bookshelf look cluttered.

6. Leave a little free space on each shelf so that books aren't packed too tightly, but not so much that they lean.

7. As an economical alternative to built-ins, line a wall with several identical bookshelves painted to match the walls.

QUICK TIP: **Reach for the Heights**

Lining a wall with shelves subtracts as little as fifteen inches from a room yet creates yards of storage for books and other possessions.

149 Three ways to reduce book clutter

For some people, books are like trophies—a statement of achievement and a reflection of one's intellect, education, travels, and interests. A true bibliophile may find it emotionally difficult to get rid of books. If it's time to weed shelves, consider these options:

1. **Give books away.** Give a book you have already read to a friend who you know would love it. Or donate books to your local library, community center, or charitable organization.

2. **Swap.** BookMooch and PaperBack Swap are examples of online communities for exchanging used books. Users give away books for credits and then use credits to obtain other books. (Not the best for reducing clutter, but it's a good way to get books for free.)

3. **Sell.** For those who need a financial incentive to de-clutter, Amazon makes selling used books easy. Once you've set up an account, listed your books, and made a sale, Amazon will e-mail you a packing slip and shipping label. They add shipping costs automatically to the selling price and send you an electronic deposit periodically. Half.com (part of eBay) is another online venue. While old college texts and last year's bestsellers might not fetch a lot, a market always exists for such titles as big, graphic coffee table books.

150 Remembering what you've read: the life book list

It's fun to keep a record of your reading. Start a designated journal, and add books as you finish them. Or use a computer spreadsheet, which will allow you to organize the list in different ways, such as by date for a historical record or by book title for easy reference. Include the author's name and genre. Or do it virtually with Goodreads (www.goodreads.com), a free social cataloging and networking site. Goodreads provides users with three "shelves"—books you've read, books you are currently reading, and books you want to read—and you can add your own shelves to suit your own tastes. Connect to friends to see what they are reading. You can also write reviews, contact authors, and post books that you'd like to swap or sell (a great way to reduce book clutter).

151 All the news that fits

Don't let newspapers pile up. Designate a place where newspapers will go (on a tray, in a magazine rack, a basket, etc.), and when they no longer fit, it's time to move them to the recycling bin. Another rule of thumb is to keep only the current day's paper and the Sunday paper from last week. Remember that you can always find back articles online.

152 How to create a clippings file

If you need to read an article in yesterday's paper, cut it out and put it in a "Rip & Read" folder. Take this folder along when you are likely to have idle waiting time, such as a doctor's appointment, a kid's music lesson, or the line at the post office.

Another option is to use your computer as a filing cabinet for magazine information. Simply scan articles, save them to your hard drive, and then recycle the paper. (See entry 176, "PDFs and scanning demystified," and entry 195, "Computer filing strategies.") Or try Scanalog (www.scanalog.com), a magazine cataloguing software program that gives you an attractive interface to store and retrieve articles and catalog them by any subject.

153 Managing magazines

Organizing guru Peter Walsh suggests subscribing to only three magazines per person and keeping no more than three issues of a single magazine at any one time. That means magazines should be in continuous motion—as a new one comes in, the oldest issue must go. If you are saving a magazine (or stack of magazines) because of an article or idea you want to reference, tear out the relevant pages and file them in a "Rip & Read" folder (see previous entry). If you plan on saving the article for future reference, create files for your top five interests and keep them in the filing cabinet. Examples are travel ideas, kids' activities, and remodeling and decorating. Make sure they are files that you will actively reference and that the information remains timely. If you do need to save back issues of a magazine (for business or other purposes), then keep them tidy and protected in a magazine file on a shelf.

154 On display

Try these ideas for displaying a collection:

- Grouped items make more of an impact. Use walls, shelves, mantel, or end table, whatever will best "frame" your collection.
- You don't need to display your entire collection at once. Choose only your favorites to display, or if you have many great pieces, rotate your collection.
- Group items that are the same color to make a visual statement.
- Arrange objects in odd numbers to create visual tension and interest.
- Coordinate items to complement the collection. For instance, a stack of coffee table books about vintage Bakelite radios can provide a pedestal for one.

To turn your magazine collection into one or several reference volumes, take a tip from libraries and send the set to an archival book-binding service, which will produce hardcovers for about fifty dollars per two-inch-thick book. Title, volumes, and year are printed on the spine.

155   How to safeguard your collections

If items in your collection are valuable, you will want to protect them against loss.

To safeguard your objects, make sure you have:

- An inventory list. Maintaining an inventory of your collection, including the original receipts, will help document the value of your collection and expedite a claim in the event of a loss. Keep a copy of the inventory and receipts in a location separate from your actual collection (such as a safe-deposit box).
- Photographs. Photos will provide further proof of the contents in your collection. Be sure to photograph any markings (stamps, signatures, etc.) that will help prove the authenticity of the piece.
- Insurance. Since most homeowner's insurance policies allow only limited coverage on collectibles, you might consider adding another policy that will cover your valuable collectibles from loss due to theft, fire, breakage, flooding, and natural disasters. Insurance companies that specialize in collectibles offer less-expensive policies than homeowner policy add-ons.

living rooms and dens

156   Toy story

If your family room looks more like the set of *Romper Room,* then you need to create storage solutions for toys, games, and crafts.

- **Large toys:** use a wide and fairly shallow container. Kids should be able to reach for a toy on the bottom without too much trouble. A wooden chest or rattan basket can function as well-disguised receptacles for toys.
- **Small toys:** for blocks, Matchbox cars, and tea party essentials, use clear, lidded plastic storage boxes and store them on shelves inside a larger storage piece such as an armoire or TV unit. Use identical boxes that will stack well and give a uniform look. Label the boxes with a label maker or, especially for younger children, with pictures of what's inside.

157   Other toy storage ideas

- Outfit lower shelves of a bookcase with canvas baskets or storage cubes to house and conceal small toys and books. Younger kids can easily pull the whole container off the shelf to access toys.
- Store games, puzzles, and cards on shelves or in a drawer.
- Decide how many toys your family room can comfortably contain without intruding on adults. Store the rest in an accessible place in the garage, basement, or another storage area. Change the toys each month, keeping different toys in rotation.
- Teach children to put toys and games away after they've played with them.

158 To the dogs

Who doesn't love to spoil their dog rotten? Any box or basket can serve as a place to store dog toys. Consider whether you want your dog to have access to the toys. A box with a lid (and a snout-safe clasp!) or a taller container will enable *you* to parcel out toys and control how many are in rotation (i.e., scattered all over the house) at once. A shorter box without a lid gives your pooch the freedom to empty the box as he/she is moved to do so. Some dogs can even be trained to put toys *back* in the box when done.

INSTANT GUEST BED

Make room for guests with convertible furniture. Of course, a sofa bed can transform into a berth, but armchairs and ottomans can, too. Or choose a simple storage ottoman and keep an inflatable Aerobed inside.

QUICK TIP: **Collecting Software**

A number of cataloging software programs on the market let you catalog your collection(s). Collectify (www.collectify.com) is one that I have found affordable, flexible, and easy to use. It allows you to create a detailed database (with photos) to document everything about the objects in your collection, including the purchase date and price, vendor, provenance, markings, location in your home (or elsewhere), restoration costs, etc.

living rooms and dens

159 Trays: the most useful accessory

A versatile addition to any family room or living room, a tray can serve a multitude of functions. Plus it's easy to whisk things out of sight whenever necessary. Some *tray* chic ideas:

- Fashion a coffee table out of an ottoman by resting a tray atop one. Use it to hold candles or a vase of flowers.
- Place a tray on a sideboard table to hold a stack of current magazines or bar items.
- Store remote controls on a tray on the coffee table.
- Create an end table, using a tray as the tabletop. Make the base out of a stack of books, a luggage stand, or a stool.
- Use a tray to display a collection.

160 Five steps to organizing photographs

While most photography is now done digitally, many of us still have a collection of old film-processed photos to organize. Get the job done by following these steps:

1. **Gather.** Collect photos from everywhere in the house into a central sorting location.

2. **Edit.** Immediately eliminate photos that are out of focus, unflattering, overexposed or underexposed, or have a thumb or camera strap in the way. Get rid of duplicates (give them to Grandma) or at least photos that are redundant (choose the best of those eighteen Eiffel Tower shots).

3. **Sort.** Go through packets of loose photos and sort them as best you can by year. After that, sort the years chronologically into seasons (summer 2005) or specific events (Junior's eighth birthday party). To help keep sorted piles of loose photos organized, put them in transparent plastic sleeves with a sticky note indicating the year until you are ready to transfer them into boxes.

4. **Label.** If photos are in the developer's envelope, label the envelope with the occasion or season and date. Stick loose photos in an envelope and label that. If you want to label individual loose photos, use a no. 2 pencil to write on the back of the photo.

5. **Contain.** A typical photo storage box can accommodate more than a thousand loose four-by-six photos. For long-term storage and preservation, look for acid- or lignin-free boxes (available at camera and photo supply stores), which protect photos from fading, yellowing, and disintegrating. Choosing identical storage boxes in one or two colors will create a uniform look on a shelf. For a more economical way to go, repurpose shoe boxes for the occasion, uniting them with matching labels.

Work Smart
The Home Office

For many people, the home office is becoming the sole office. But even if you work outside the home, it's essential to have an appointed place in your home for conducting household business, whether it is in a separate room, a converted closet, or a desk in the kitchen. Don't let your home office get bogged down with paper pileup or an unruly desktop.

161 Filing 101

Smooth operators

Old-fashioned filing cabinets are still the easiest way to manage
a great deal of paper in an economical amount of space. The most
important feature in a filing cabinet is drawers that slide open
smoothly. Don't skimp on quality. A top-quality filing cabinet will
last for decades. Look for:

- Full-extension gliding drawers. These should have high sides to
  accommodate hanging files.
- Weighted bottom. This prevents tipping over if two drawers are
  open at once.
- Legal conversion bar. An essential for legal-size papers.

File savvy

The most effective filing systems employ a combination of hanging
files, manila file folders, and clear plastic tabs. Here are some tricks
of the trade:

- Put plastic tabs on the *front* of hanging files for easier viewing.
  Use clear three-and-a-half-inch plastic tabs, which are easy to
  read and accommodate longer file names. (Neatly write labels by
  hand, or create them with a label maker.) Tabs should be placed
  along either the left or right side of the hanging files, whichever
  side is closest to where you sit.
- Replace paper clips with staples where possible—paper clips tend
  to attach onto other papers, especially in crowded files.
- Keep file drawers less than full. If the filing cabinet gets too
  stuffed, there will be psychological resistance to using it and things
  will pile up.
- Keep a supply of hanging and manila folders in a convenient place.
  If a logical place doesn't exist for a document, make a new file.
  Extra tabs and labels should be kept in a handy drawer or desktop
  organizer.

- In a simple home office filing system, separate financial files from personal files. Financial files include credit card statements, utility bills, car payments, taxes, receipts, insurance bills, medical bills, charitable contributions, investments, etc. Personal files include important documents such as birth and marriage certificates, memorabilia, owner's manuals, insurance policies, medical records (as opposed to medical *bills*), and information regarding kids, cars, pets, and hobbies. If you work at home, you'll want to set up separate drawers for work files.
- Clean out your files at least once a year.
- Create folders for personal categories, such as hobbies or interests. I had a client who had the habit of ripping pictures of hairdos that she liked out of magazines. She had a filing system in place, but she thought of it as a way to manage life's serious matters like bills and insurance. We set up a file called HAIRDOS and created a place to corral all these tear sheets. What is your "hairdo" equivalent?

FILE FURNITURE

Traditional filing cabinets have a decidedly functional aesthetic. To integrate one into your decor, look for filing cabinets that resemble (and double as) furniture, such as file storage consoles or ottomans.

162 Paper in and out

Create this three-tiered system to keep papers organized and moving across your desk:

1. In-box. This is a place to capture miscellaneous documents that have not yet been organized, including mail to read, invitations to respond to, forms to fill out, etc. Evaluate the contents of your in-box each day. Remove in-box items one at a time. Determine what needs to be done and do it.

2. Action files. Action files are a way to manage documents that are either in process or can't be handled immediately (such as filing and following up on insurance claims), or current projects that need to be tackled (such as deciding on fixtures for the bathroom renovation or filling out school forms). If action files are filed in a drawer, chances are you'll forget about them. Keep them in a tray on the desk, or if you need to see them at a glance, put them in a desktop file sorter or stepped file. When projects are complete, file only papers you'll need to refer to again.

3. Out-box. Assign a place on your desk for completed items such as outgoing mail. A two-tiered tray can serve as an in-box (top) and out-box (bottom).

163 Filers versus pilers

It's some people's nature to file, and others to pile. Filers have no trouble keeping files in drawers, pulling them out as needed. Pilers, on the other hand, are wary of filing things for fear of forgetting that they exist. If you are a piler, even the most superior filing system might not serve your needs. As an alternative to filing cabinets, try using a system of boxes or baskets, lined up on shelves within reach of your desk. Label them with categories pertaining to your personal and professional life, such as bills, insurance claims, expense receipts, and invitations. Boxes should be large enough to fit the contents, but no so deep that they become an abyss. Use filing cabinets for long-term storage of important papers that you are required to save.

QUICK TIP: **Shredding Savvy**

The Federal Trade Commission estimates that 10 million Americans are victims of identity theft each year. To protect yourself from identity theft, shred any document that contains sensitive information such as your signature, account numbers, Social Security number, date of birth, driver's license number, or any medical, financial, or legal information. For a complete list of documents to shred, visit www.fightidentitytheft.com. Bonus: use shredded paper as packing material instead of environment-polluting Styrofoam peanuts or plastic bubble wrap.

164 Drowning in paper?
Use this *R-A-F-T*

There are four actions one can take with any document:

Refer it. If someone else can or should handle it, give it to them. If you need to follow up later, put a note on your to-do list, in your calendar, or in your tickler file.

Act on it. Process the document. Pay the bill. Do what needs to be done.

File it. If you need to save paperwork, file it in the appropriate folder. If there's no clear place for it, create a new file.

Toss it. (See entry 166, "When to toss: documents.")

QUICK TIP: **Overcoming Indecision**

Decide comes from the Latin *occido,* meaning "to kill." It is the same root found in *homicide, suicide,* and *pesticide. De* means "two." When we make a decision, we are cutting something in two and killing whatever we decide against. It's this idea (whether we are aware of it or not) of killing off other options that makes decision making difficult for some people. Sometimes simply recognizing this makes indecision easier to overcome.

165 Tickle your memory

A tickler file is a reminder system for time-sensitive papers that require follow-up action. Productivity guru David Allen popularized this in his acclaimed book *Getting Things Done,* as a helpful way to "tickle" your memory. To create a traditional tickler file, use an accordion folder with forty-three pockets, thirty-one for the days of the month plus twelve for the months of the year. File papers in the pocket corresponding to the day you need to follow up. If the follow-up date falls after the current month, write the date in the upper right-hand corner of the paper and file it in the folder for the corresponding month. At the beginning of each month, take the papers from that pocket and distribute them accordingly. A tickler file can also serve as a place to put papers that you'll need on a future date but don't know what to do with in the meantime. For instance, use it to hold concert or theater tickets, forms you need to take to a doctor's appointment, or directions to an event. The tickler file is an amazingly productive organization tool, as long as you get in the habit of checking it every day.

166 When to toss: documents

If you aren't sure what to throw away, ask yourself the following questions:

- Is the information current and relevant and will it be by the time I need to reference it? If not, toss.
- Can I foresee a specific circumstance where I would need this information? If not, toss.
- Would this information be difficult to find again? If not, toss. Many records, including bank statements, are now available online.
- Am I really going to get around to this? Be honest. If not, toss.
- Is this a tax or legal document? (See entry 173, "What do I save for taxes and for how long?")

167 The daily mail

To combat paper pileup, make a habit of sorting your mail every day. Follow these steps:

1. Upon collecting the mail, sort out the junk and throw it away. Keep a trash can in your entryway for this purpose.

2. Set the mail down in its appointed place, a tray in the kitchen or entryway, until you are ready to deal with it.

3. When ready to process the mail, separate it into categories:

   - Put magazines and catalogs in a magazine rack.
   - Put bills in a bill organizer that is front and center on your desk. A thirty-one-day bill organizer will help ensure that bills get paid on time.
   - Keep other items requiring action, including things to be filed or that need a response, in an in-box on your desk and tackle one item at a time. (See entry 162, "Paper in and out.")

If you are in the habit of printing information that you find online, consider using bookmarks instead. Most Web browsers allow you to easily organize your favorite Web sites the way you would files on your computer. For instance, create a bookmark folder called SCHEDULES for train and bus schedules. This is one way to cut down on unnecessary paper and to ensure that you have the most up-to-date information.

168 Online bill-paying

Paying bills via computer will:

- Save time. It takes less time to log in and pay bills than it does to write out checks and address envelopes.
- Save money. When you pay bills online, you don't need stamps.
- Reduce paper. Opt to receive bills via e-mail for even less waste.
- Save the environment. Save trees as well as the energy needed to collect, process, transport, and deliver your mail.

If you don't already pay your bills online, set it up through your bank's online bill payment Web site. This will make bill paying a one-stop endeavor. Decide what days of the month you would like to pay your bills, and then contact your accounts and request that your bills be due on the dates you've chosen. You can opt to split bills in half and pay them twice a month. One option is to receive bills via e-mail. Set up a folder in your e-mail inbox for online bills, and pay them at least a week before the due dates. Print out only the front page of bills you need for tax purposes. Or set up automatic payments from your checking account.

the home office

169 How to file paid bills

Invest in a twelve-pocket January to December accordion folder. Take your paid bills for the month and put them in the corresponding pocket. After twelve months, take out the oldest bills to make room for the new ones, and unless you need to save them for your taxes, throw them out. If you write off some of your expenses, keep two separate accordion folders, one for personal bills you don't need to save, and another for business-related bills and expenses, which should be labeled and saved at the end of the year with other tax data.

170 Saving receipts

You will need two systems—one for business and one for personal receipts.

- Business. Collect monthly receipts in a letter-size envelope. Write the month and year on the front and assign a place for it on your desk (or keep the envelope in a handbag or computer bag as an easy way to collect receipts while on the go). At the end of the month, record your expenses using accounting software such as QuickBooks. File the envelope in a twelve-month accordion folder with your paid business bills. Start a new envelope for the next month.
- Personal. It's essential to save receipts for home improvements and important purchases such as appliances, computers, electronics, jewelry, art, antiques, and furniture. Give each category a labeled manila folder and store them inside hanging files with a tab labeled RECEIPTS—PERSONAL inside your filing drawer. In the case of jewelry, art, and antiques, organizing receipts eases the process of insuring them. Save receipts for as long as you own the item.

171 Medical bills and insurance claims

There are five steps to filing insurance claims:

1. Pay bills. Keep medical bills that need to be paid on your desk with your other bills.

2. Submit claims. Put paid bills in a folder entitled CLAIMS TO SUBMIT and keep it on your desk. Schedule time as needed to submit claims, making a copy of each bill you submit.

3. File submitted claims. Once you have submitted the claims, staple a copy of the bill to the claim form and place it in a file in your file drawer labeled SUBMITTED CLAIMS.

4. Check claims against explanation of benefits (EOBs). When EOBs arrive in the mail, check them against the submitted claims. If you need to keep the paperwork (for example, if you claim medical expenses on your tax return), staple the EOBs to the claims and file under COMPLETED CLAIMS. Otherwise, once a claim is completed, you can discard the paperwork.

5. Dispute benefits. If there is a discrepancy that you need to take up with the insurance company, staple the paid bill to the EOB and put it in a folder called INSURANCE DISPUTES on the desk. Schedule time to call about your disputes.

172 Keeping important documents

Store hard-to-replace documents, such as birth certificates, titles, deeds, marriage licenses, divorce documents, etc., in a safe-deposit box, and keep copies in a personal file drawer called IMPORTANT DOCUMENTS. If you choose to keep these documents at home, invest in a fireproof safe to protect them against loss. Home safes are rated based on the number of hours contents will be protected from a fire's heat. A one-hour rating (which means that the safe was tested for one hour at a heat two to three times hotter than the average fire) is sufficient for household use.

Scanning important documents and saving them as PDFs (See entry 176, "PDFs and scanning demystified") ensures that you can instantly produce a copy if needed.

173 What do I save for taxes and for how long?

According to Frederic H. Lerner, a professor of financial management at New York University, if you and a partner file either a joint tax return or individual tax returns, then each of you should retain the following documents. Use this as a general reference, but consult with your accountant for any unique requirements you might have.

RECORD RETENTION GUIDELINES FOR BUSINESS

Save until updated
• Chart of accounts

Save for 2 years
• Bank reconciliations

Save for 7 years
• Accounts payable
• Accounts receivable
• Audit reports
• Bank statements
• Cancelled checks
• Chart of accounts
• Electronic payment records
• Expense records
• Financial statements (Y/E)
• General ledger
• Loan payment schedules
• Purchase orders (1 copy)
• Sales records
• Tax returns

Save until fully depreciated or sold
• Depreciation schedules
• Fixed asset purchases

Save permanently
• Cancelled checks for real-estate purchases
• Inventory records (if using LIFO system)
• Tax returns if criminal fraud is involved

RECORD RETENTION GUIDELINES FOR INDIVIDUALS

Save for 7 years
• 1099s
• Bank deposit slips
• Bank statements
• Brokerage statements (Y/E)
• Cancelled checks supporting tax deductions
• Charitable contribution documentation
• Credit card statements
• IRA nondeductible contributions
• Receipts, diaries, logs pertaining to tax return
• Tax returns (if uncomplicated)
• W-2s

Save for warranty period of the item
• Home repair receipts & cancelled checks

Save for term of loan/policy or until maturity + 3 years
• Insurance policy
• IRA annual reports
• Loans
• Mutual fund annual statements

Save for ownership period + 7 years
• Dividend reinvestment records
• Home improvement receipts & cancelled checks
• Investment property purchase documents
• Investment purchase & sales slips

Save permanently
• Divorce documents
• Estate planning documents (most recent version)
• Retirement plan annual reports
• Tax returns (if complicated)

174 How to impress your accountant at tax time

In a file drawer, create a hanging folder called TAXES.
Use manila folders for each of the following tax-
related documents: year-end statements, tax forms (for
wages, miscellaneous income, interest income, etc.),
deductions, estimated taxes, property taxes, and any
other tax documents you receive. As tax forms come
in, file them accordingly. At tax time, simply bring
the preorganized manila folders to your accountant
along with any other relevant income and expense
documentation. Reuse the folders every year.

175 The paper-*less* office

To reduce the paper in your home office, try these tools:

Electronic invoices and online bill payment. Ask credit card and utility companies to invoice you electronically so you can pay bills online. (See entry 168, "Online bill-paying.")

Electronic faxing. Use a service like efax.com, which lets you generate outgoing faxes on the computer and send them through the Internet. Incoming faxes are delivered to your e-mail in-box.

Scanner and shredder. Don't worry about scanning old records, since after seven years, most of what you have to save for tax purposes can be thrown out. Scan and shred as much of your *current* paper as you can and file the documents on your computer. (See entry 195, "Computer filing strategies.") Keep in mind that most credit-card and utility companies as well as banks will make seven years of statements available online.

External hard drive. When storing information electronically, regular, consistent, and reliable backup is a must. (See entry 193, "Safeguarding data.")

QUICK TIP: **Web Site Passwords**

Create an e-mail folder for online subscriptions and Web site passwords. Anytime you subscribe to a Web site and choose a username you will get a confirmation e-mail. File these in the same folder so that when you revisit a Web site that requires you to sign in, you'll have easy access to password information on hand.

what's a disorganized person to do?

176 PDFs and scanning demystified

A PDF, or Portable Document Format, is an electronic snapshot of a document. You can create a PDF from documents created in any program. A PDF preserves the fonts, layout, graphics, and images and is accessible on any computer even without the program that created the original document, the same operating system, the relevant fonts, or other elements. You can create a PDF of a scanned hard copy, a Web page, or any printable electronic file.

How to make a PDF

To create PDFs, you must first download Adobe Acrobat, which is available for free at www.adobe.com. To save any printable document as a PDF file, in the File menu, click *Print*. In the Print dialogue box, look for a PDF button and then *Save as PDF*.

How to Scan

To scan documents, check the specific instructions in your scanner's manual, but generally speaking, place the document on the scanner bed and close the lid. Open your scanning software and select *Acquire* or *Import* from the File menu. Click *Preview* to create an image of what is on the bed onto the screen. With the mouse, highlight the area you want to scan. Select the resolution, which is measured in dpi, or dots per inch. (Sometimes you will see ppi, pixels per inch, which is the same thing.) A dpi of 72 is sufficient for scanning documents. Click the *Scan* button and wait 15 to 60 seconds for the scanner to produce an acquired image. Choose *Save as* from the File menu to name the page and save the image as a PDF document into the relevant folder. (See entry 195, "Computer filing strategies.")

177   Manuals and warranties

Use one of these two methods for saving owner's manuals, warranties, big-ticket-item receipts, and contacts for repairs:

1. Folders. Divide manuals into the following categories: appliances, cameras, computers (including software and peripherals like printers and hard drives), electronics, household, kids' stuff, kitchen, and phones. File them in your personal file drawer.

2. Binders. If you prefer to keep manuals near where you use the products, create a binder. For instance, use a three-hole punch on all the kitchen gadget and appliance manuals and keep them in a three-ring binder in the kitchen so that when the refrigerator is on the fritz, you can quickly locate the instruction manual.

QUICK TIP: **Check for a PDF**

Many manuals are available on company Web sites as PDFs. If what you need is available online, you can create a manuals folder on your computer and recycle your paper versions, reducing manual pileup.

178   Junk mail

There are several ways to combat junk mail. Catalog Choice (www.catalogchoice.org) is a service that lets you "unsubscribe" to catalogs you don't want. Filling out a form at www.donotmail.org will take you off the lists of several major junk mail offenders. You can also call 888-5-OPT-OUT (888-567-8688) to stop receiving unwanted credit card solicitations. You will have to provide your name, address, previous address, and Social Security number.

For a low annual fee, Tonic Mailstopper (http://mailstopper.tonic .com) will automatically remove your name from junk mail lists and monitor lists on a monthly basis to keep your name from reappearing. You can cancel catalogs you don't want to receive, and the company also plants trees in your honor to help the environment.

Bear in mind that names, addresses, and buying habits are regularly traded on the open market. There is nothing to stop a company from selling yours, but these steps will help to reduce the volume of junk mail and solicitations:

• When ordering a product or service or donating money via mail or over the phone, specify verbally or in writing that you do not want your information sold or traded to other companies. Most organizations will respect your wishes.
• Product warranty cards are often used to collect information on your buying habits for direct mail purposes. Read the fine print to see if warranty cards are actually required to validate the warranty. If not, think twice about mailing them in.
• Avoid filling out entry forms for "contests," as these are often a ruse for gathering consumer data.

179 Reduce telemarketing calls

Register with the National Do Not Call Registry to stop telemarketers from calling you at home or on your mobile phone. Once your number has been on the registry for thirty-one days, telemarketers should not call. If they do, you can file a complaint on the Web site. Thanks to the Do-Not-Call Improvement Act of 2007, numbers placed on the National Do Not Call Registry will remain on it permanently. You can register online for free at www.donotcall.gov or by calling 888-382-1222 from the number you want to register.

180 Customer service: how to get a human on the phone

Bookmark www.get2human.com in your Web browser and save yourself hours of unnecessary aggravation. This Web site has compiled a database of secret phone numbers and codes that immediately get you to an actual live customer service *person* at a thousand major companies. The site also has a Great Customer Service Club, where consumers rate customer service. Feedback is organized by industry to help consumers choose companies with superior customer service.

181 Ten things you should shred

Shred anything containing personal information such as your name, Social Security number, phone number, account numbers, signature, and medical or legal information. Specifically, shred the following:

1. Preapproved credit offers and applications

2. Expired debit and credit cards (many shredders can handle plastic cards)

3. Credit card statements and receipts

4. Bank account statements and cancelled checks

5. Investment account statements

6. Paycheck stubs

7. Utility and phone bills

8. Insurance policy information and claims

9. Tax returns

10. Expired passports (after getting a renewal) and ID cards

Check entry 173, "What do I save for taxes and for how long?" to find out when you can safely shred tax-related documents.

182 The minimalist desktop

Pare down the items on your desk to the following necessities:

• In-box, action files, and out-box
• Computer and peripherals
• Holder for pens, scissors, and letter opener
• Holder for bills
• Stapler and tape dispenser
• Label maker (you can also keep this on a shelf nearby)
• Master notebook (see entry 187, "A master notebook")
• One decorative object

No drawers?

If you don't have drawer space in your desk, make space for the things that would normally go in them. Small containers on the desk can hold paper clips, a roll of stamps, extra staples. Lidded boxes on shelves can serve as auxiliary drawers. Figure out categories of things you need to store and put them in a labeled box on a shelf. (See entry 186, "Organize office supplies.")

183 One-Hour Project
Organize your desk drawers

- Take everything out of the drawer(s).
- Discard the junk . . . old Post-it notes, ATM receipts, broken rubber bands, etc.
- Relocate things that belong elsewhere such as photos or a stray bank statement.
- Group like items together to see what you have. Desk drawers should be used only for things that support you in getting paperwork, projects, and phone calling done.
- Furnish shallow drawers with organizers to divide space. Choose drawer organizers with individual components so you can outfit your drawer with the appropriate size boxes to contain what you are storing—small compartments for paper clips, larger ones for camera and cell phone USB cables.
- Keep small things in shallow drawers. Big pads of paper, envelopes, and spare manila folders will obstruct what's in the drawers. Better to store these on a shelf. (See entry 186, "Organize office supplies.")

To keep track of all those "notes to self," try Evernote (www.evernote.com), a free note-taking application that synchronizes all the info you enter among your computer, phone, and the Web. Speak your brainstorm into the audio recorder, or type the title of a recommended book into a list of books to read. Snap a photo of the label on a tasty bottle of wine, or the Realtor sign in front of your dream house. Sync to let notes created on your phone be viewed on your computer and vice versa so that information is always at hand.

184 Combat cord clutter

To neaten an unsightly jumble of cords on the floor of your office, bundle loose cords together using plastic cord ties. Or improvise with what you have around the house such as pipe cleaners, twist ties, or rubber bands. Color code plugs and cords with colored stick-on file labels and matching sticker dots to make it easy to identify and reconnect equipment. Use cord concealers to corral and hide cords. If you want to make them disappear altogether, use strips of Velcro to attach a surge protector and the accompanying bundled wires to the underside of your desk.

185   Hire a virtual assistant

Need help but don't have the budget for a personal assistant? Try a virtual assistant. These entrepreneurs provide administrative, technical, creative, or personal support to clients from a remote location, usually their own home office. A virtual assistant can help with ongoing aspects of home or business life such as bill paying and bookkeeping; short-term work projects like holiday mailings; or work related to a single aspect of your business, such as Web design or marketing. Communication and delivery of services is done primarily via phone, e-mail, and over the Internet. For ongoing administrative support, visit http://AssistU.com. For short-term projects, such as bookkeeping or Web design, find referrals at www.elance.com.

186   Organize office supplies

Even without a closet or cabinet to dedicate to office supplies, it's easy to create an effective organizing system with just a small amount of counter or shelf space. Group your supplies into categories. For instance, you might need to store envelopes, printer paper, notepads, computer cables, ink cartridges, or replacement supplies (like boxes of staples or paper clips). Put each category in a lidded box and label the outside of the box. Add a design element by choosing one color and acquiring boxes of different sizes in that color.

187 A master notebook

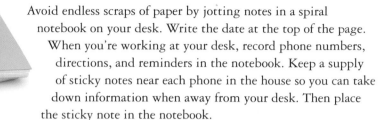

Avoid endless scraps of paper by jotting notes in a spiral notebook on your desk. Write the date at the top of the page. When you're working at your desk, record phone numbers, directions, and reminders in the notebook. Keep a supply of sticky notes near each phone in the house so you can take down information when away from your desk. Then place the sticky note in the notebook.

188 How to remember birthdays and other important dates

Low-tech. Keep a list. Write the name of each month and under it, write the date and the name of the celebrant(s). Keep the list where you'll see it often, such as on a bulletin board or the fridge.

Medium-tech. Input birthdays into your smartphone calendar. Most calendars have an alert option that you can set to notify you ahead of time.

High-tech. Use an online birthday notification service such as birthdayalarm.com or plaxo.com. Weekly Facebook birthday reminders are handy, too.

THE OFFICE/ GUESTROOM

With thoughtful design, an office and a guest bedroom can peacefully coexist. When designing such a room, minimalism is key, as you'll want to be able to stow work away when guests are using the room and also provide space for them to unpack their belongings. A computer armoire with file drawers and shelf space is an easy way to hide the computer, files, and office supplies. A built-in desk can provide extra workspace and also serve as a dressing table for guests. A second armoire can double as an entertainment unit and provide drawer space for spare bedding or a guest's clothes. A trundle bed is the perfect daybed/couch that can roll out to accommodate a second guest. A number of furniture companies are producing thoughtfully designed small-space solutions such as desks with components that rearrange to reveal a bed.

189 Get a grip on greeting cards

There are two categories of greeting cards. The ones you receive and the ones you plan to give.

• **The ones you receive:** Save only cards with real sentimental value to you. Toss cards from your newspaper delivery boy and dentist, then sort the rest by sender (e.g., "spouse," "kids," and "friends & family"). Invest in a few matching colored boxes, label them, and stack them on a shelf out in the open so it's easy to file the keepers away.

• **The ones you give:** Buying cards in advance of birthdays and holidays can save you the stress of having to pick one up at the last minute. In order to locate what you need when the time comes, make a greeting card organizer. Buy a three-ring binder and insert heavyweight, top-loading, clear plastic sheet protectors. Use tab dividers to delineate card categories such as birthdays, kids' birthdays, anniversaries, get well, sympathy, thank you, various holidays, and blank cards. Insert new cards in the respective sheet protectors so you have an organized stash when occasions arise. Label the spine and store the binder on a shelf. Another option is a "card catalog" with dividers to separate by category.

190 Keeping track of invitations

After you've responded yes to an invitation, enter it into your calendar immediately along with the salient details, including address and dress code. If you've RSVP'd for your partner, communicate the date and details to him or her. If there is too much information to transfer into your calendar (such as directions), post the invitation on your bulletin board or file the invitation in a tickler file under the date of the event. (See entry 165, "Tickle your memory.")

190 Should I keep the computer box?

No. Once you've discovered that your computer's in working order and you've decided to keep it, throw out the box, but cut out the serial number printed on the box, write the name of the computer on the back, and store it with your owner's manuals. The same goes for most appliance boxes, save for those items you use only occasionally and need to store safely.

192 Work Healthy

An ergonomically correct desk setup can help you avoid backaches, eye strain, and fatigue. Arrange your home office setup for optimum benefit:

- **The height is right.** The computer screen should sit eighteen to twenty-two inches away from your face, with the center of the screen about ten to fifteen degrees below your eyes.
- **Mind your posture.** Maintain the proper body position: Head and neck should be straight. Wrists should be unbent, forearms parallel to the floor, shoulders relaxed, elbows close to the body. The work surface should be set at elbow level. Feet should be flat on the floor or supported by a footrest. Hips should be even with or slightly higher than knees.
- **Get a good chair.** Even if you're not prone to lower back pain, choose a chair with lumbar support.
- **Avoid eye strain.** Reduce overhead lighting. If you can see your reflection or a glare in the computer screen, reposition it or reduce ambient lighting, closing blinds or curtains if bright sunlight is causing the glare.

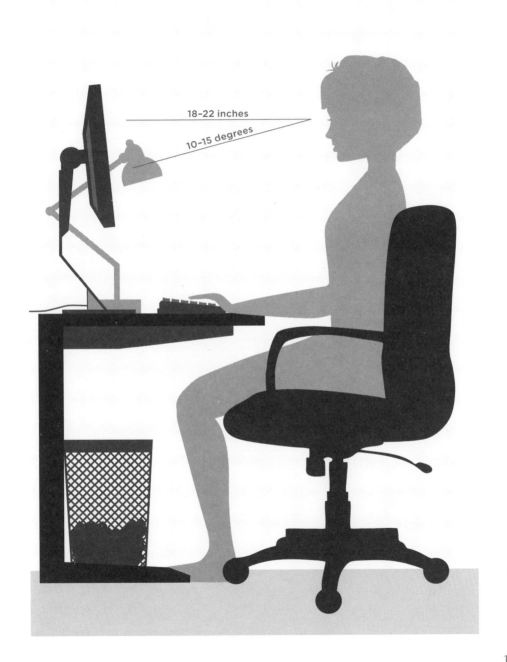

18-22 inches

10-15 degrees

193 Safeguarding data

Because we store so much valuable data and information on our computers, backing up regularly is an absolute must. You can back up your data either online or onto an external hard drive. Backing up data online protects you not only from data loss resulting from a hard drive crash, but also from fires, floods, and burglaries. With an online data backup service such as Mozy (http://www.mozy.com), you create an account, download and install their software, select the sets of data you want to back up (photos, music, e-mail, contacts, and documents), and schedule the frequency of backups. Your data is backed up automatically at regularly scheduled intervals to a remote, secure server. If you prefer to back your data up to an external hard drive, check to see if your computer has backup software installed. As long as your computer is connected to an external hard drive, it will back up your data automatically, running in the background so as not to disturb your work. If your computer doesn't have a built-in program, choose an external hard drive that comes with backup software.

194 Are online data backup services safe?

Generally speaking, online data backup services are safe, but since you are entrusting your data to an outside party, it is important to choose a reputable and reliable provider. Things to look for:

• Competent and accessible tech support
• Ease of restoring data
• High-security measures including
   - encryption of data during transfer

- password-protected account access
- firewalls to keep out intruders
- backup generators to keep data accessible during a power outage
- a secure building to house the data center

Keep in mind that data stored online is accessible to you only when you have an Internet connection. For critical information, consider using multiple methods of backup such as an external hard drive in addition to an online server.

195 Computer filing strategies

Keep as little on your computer desktop as possible. Use your computer's Documents folder like a filing cabinet. All files go inside labeled folders and all folders go in the filing cabinet (the Documents folder). Take some extra time to design a folder system that will make it easy to *find* what you are looking for rather than easy to *save*. A simple system is usually more effective than a labyrinth of folders. Start with broad category folders covering the different aspects of your personal and business life and then create relevant folders under each one. Try these categories:

- Paperwork and bills. Any documentation that comes to you electronically such as bank and credit card statements, utility bills, and tax or insurance documents.
- Personal information. Your current resume, a list of credit card numbers and corresponding customer service numbers (in case of loss), and PDF copies of passport, driver's license, social security card, birth certificate, etc. Password-protect this folder to keep data safe.
- Projects and work. Organized by job (or client) or personal project.
- Reading. Material generated by someone else such as articles downloaded from the Internet, PDF books, etc.

- **Writing.** Personal material generated by you such as letters, notes, invitations, creative writing, journal entries, etc.
- **Interests.** Could be recipes, sheet music, your daughter's sketches, etc.

QUICK TIP: **Desktop Shortcut**

To go straight to the desktop without having to minimize and/or resize windows, click the Windows key+D on a PC and the F11 key on a Mac (fn key+F11 for older operating systems).

196 Six ways to optimize your PC's performance

According to New York–based technology consultant John Bogosian, if your PC seems lethargic, these six tips will enable it to start up and run more efficiently:

1. Add memory. You should have at least 1G of RAM, but 2G is optimal.

2. Run system updates. Configure Automatic Updates in your Control Panel to enable your computer to download operating system updates as they become available. Also, subscribe to Microsoft Updates, which installs patches to your Microsoft Office applications (Word, Excel, etc.).

3. Clean up spyware. Spyware threats range from programs that report your Websurfing activity to marketers, to those that capture credit card and other information as you type. Clean up existing spyware and get preemptive protection from future attacks with a program such as Windows Defender (available as a free download from www.microsoft.com/windows/downloads/).

4. **Remove temporary files and background services.** Download CCleaner, a freeware system optimization and privacy tool that will remove temporary files that are taking up disk space and may be slowing down your Web browsing. When you launch CCleaner, make sure that you uncheck *Empty Recycle Bin, Cookies, History,* and other items that you may not want cleaned.

5. **Change your Visual Performance Settings.** If you can live without the pretty window borders, transition effects, rounded corners, and colored themes that come with Windows, you can get a lot of zing from changing the way your system handles visual effects. Right-click on My Computer, click on *Properties* and then the *Advanced* tab, and in the first Performance panel, click *Settings.* In the pop-up window, simply click *Adjust for Best Performance* and then *OK.*

6. **Defragment.** When your hard drive begins to fill up, data gets fragmented or broken up and stored in different parts of the drive. The computer's central processing unit (CPU) takes a longer time to process the data, which must be collected from various locations. Defragmenting is the process of rejoining the separated files. After running CCleaner, uninstalling outdated programs, emptying the trash, and getting rid of any other files you don't need, then defragment. Go to My Computer and right-click. Choose *Manage* and then *Disk Defragmenter.* Click *Analyze* to see if you need to defragment and if so, click *Defragment.*

A Note on Security Suites: Internet security suites such as McAfee and Norton—which bundle antivirus, antispyware, and antispam products into one package—are notorious for slowing down computers. Uninstalling and reinstalling may fix the problem, as will keeping subscriptions current. Some computer experts argue that Internet security suites are overkill for the home computer user and recommend going à la carte instead with Windows Firewall (turn it on in the Control Panel) plus an antivirus software. Consult with a technology expert to find out what level of protection is right for you.

If an offer for free spyware or antivirus software pops up on your screen, never install it, as it is probably some form of spyware itself. Only download software from trusted sources such as download.com.

197 Seven ways to reduce e-mail overload

To reduce unnecessary distractions in your e-mail in-box:

1. Set up spam filters. De-spam your in-box by setting up spam filters to block e-mails containing phrases like "prescription meds," "Viagra," and "replica watches."

2. Use rules. Use your e-mail program's Rules to automatically send certain e-mails into folders. For example, if you subscribe to e-mail newsletters create an e-mail folder called "To Read" and set up Rules to send them directly to that folder so that you can read the material at a later time.

3. Unsubscribe. If you are currently subscribed to e-mail newsletters or announcements that aren't in line with your current objectives and interests, unsubscribe.

4. Check for mail manually. Set your e-mail program to check for mail manually and check e-mail at appointed times only.

5. Send later. E-mailing generates more e-mail. To cut back on e-mail volume, use your e-mail program's Send Later button. If a quick response isn't required, compose e-mails and then wait until the end of the day to send them.

6. Consolidate e-mail accounts. Most computer-based e-mail programs can be configured to send and receive e-mail from

multiple e-mail accounts, Go into your e-mail Preferences, click on the Accounts tab to add e-mail accounts. Gmail is able to fetch mail from other e-mail accounts too, as long as they offer POP access (a protocol used to retrieve e-mail from a mail server), which most—but not all—do.

7. Organize your in-box. Recognize the difference between *reference* e-mails and *action* e-mails. *Action e-mails* require action on your part. If you can handle an e-mail in two minutes or less, do so to get it out of your in-box. If not, leave it there and schedule time to process e-mails one at a time. *Reference e-mails* don't require action but you need to save them for future reference. File reference e-mails in a system of folders.

QUICK TIP: **Computer Support**

At a reasonable price iyogi.com offers an annual PC support plan giving unlimited 24/7 access to technical support. Highly trained Microsoft computer engineers provide support via remote access, covering the spectrum of PC issues such as setup and installations, optimization, troubleshooting, security issues, and data backup and recovery. They also cover hardware, software, and peripherals.

Form and Function
Utility and Storage Areas

They may be purely utilitarian spaces, but a well-organized garage, tidy basement, and efficient laundry room can make the whole house run better. The key is to make the most of whatever space you have. With a little effort, the garage can be a base for outdoor activities and serve as a weekend workshop for the DIY crowd. Set up the laundry area to make this necessary chore as pleasant as possible. Transform your basement from a jumble into a storage area that works for you.

198 Sort it out

Keep a laundry basket or hamper in each bedroom or bathroom so dirty clothes are less likely to pile up on the floor. Hampers that double as laundry baskets make it easy to transport dirty clothes to the laundry room and come back filled with clean, folded clothing. If there's some extra space in the laundry area, set up a three-basket sorting system. Label it DARKS, LIGHTS, and HAND WASH, and sort accordingly. All capable family members should transport and sort their own laundry into the right bins. If space is tight, try a slim laundry sorter placed in between the washer and dryer. To maximize space, use a sorter with shelves and/or a drying rack above it.

199 Laundry soaps and cleaners

Arrange laundry detergents, fabric softeners, spot cleaners, and other laundry supplies on one shelf in order of use. Soil and stain removers on the left, followed by detergent and bleach, then fabric softener and, finally, postwashing supplies such as starches and fabric finishes. Keep all spot cleaners contained together in a basket, which can be easily pulled off the shelf to find what you are looking for. One client whose laundry room was exposed to the kitchen decanted her economy-size box of laundry powder into a clear canister along with the measuring scoop.

Keep a jackpot jar on a shelf near the washing machine for loose change and other items found in pockets.

200 Laundry room space savers

To squeeze out more space, try a:

1. Collapsible shelf. Mount collapsible metal brackets to the wall for an only-when-needed surface to fold clean clothes.

2. Slim cart. Store laundry supplies on a multitiered narrow rolling cart and stash it between the washer and dryer.

3. Wall-mounted or retractable drying line. Twelve inches from the wall is all the space needed to mount a rack to hang drying clothes. Alternately, hang a tension rod in a doorframe.

4. Fold-out ironing board. These mount to the wall or back of a door with screws. Look for the collapsible kind that folds down in a series of stages and folds back up into a compact unit.

utility and storage areas

First, try not to lose socks. One method is for each person to put dirty socks in a personalized zippered polyester mesh laundry bag. At laundry time, zipper each bag and toss it into the washing machine and dryer. It not only keeps socks together but also reduces sock-sorting time. Works for underwear and lingerie too.

Inevitably, socks will lose their mates no matter what you do. Leave them in the laundry area either in a basket, pinned to a bulletin board, or clipped to a drying wire. Then, if the missing sock reappears, it can be easily reunited with its mate. If a lost sock never resurfaces, try these novel uses for single socks.

Therapy

- **Sore muscle relief.** Put one cup of uncooked rice in a sock and tie off the end with a knot. Heat it in the microwave for thirty seconds, then apply it to sore muscles and joints. Add herbs for added aromatherapy benefit (lavender as a relaxant, eucalyptus as a decongestant, peppermint as an anti-inflammatory). Also provides relief from headaches, sinus pain, and toothaches.
- **Stress and neck pain reliever.** Tie two tennis balls together inside a sock. Lie on your back with the balls underneath your neck or head, putting pressure on either side of your cervical spine. The pressure creates deep relaxation.
- **Dry or chapped skin.** Apply olive oil liberally to dry or chapped feet and hands, and then cover them in old socks while sleeping to let the healing happen overnight without staining the sheets.

Cleaning

- **Dusting and polishing.** Slip socks on your hands to wipe blinds and ceiling fans clean. Also great for washing and waxing the car and polishing silver.
- **Defogging.** Fill a sock with salt and rub on a mirror to prevent fogging.

Fun

- **Pet toys.** Tie a knot in the middle of an old athletic sock for an instant pull toy, or put some catnip in the toe, tie a knot, and then make a ball around it with the rest of the sock.
- **Sock puppets.** Decorate using googly eyes, pipe cleaners, markers, and felt.
- **Water bottle cooler.** Freeze a bottle of water to take to the beach and put it in a sock to keep it cold longer and to prevent condensation from wetting the contents of your beach bag.
- **iPod holder.** Protect your MP3 player in a mateless sock to prevent it from getting scratched in your bag.

202 Brooms and mops

Standing mops and brooms on their heads or bristles causes them to wear out faster, but balancing them on their handles is a bit precarious. To save space, stay tidy, and keep out of the way of falling brooms, install a wall-mounted mop and broom organizer. Just press the handles into the holder to store and pull to release. Alternate heads up and down to maximize space.

203 Sewing kit essentials

No home should be without a sewing kit containing the following:

- Thread—at minimum black, white, beige, brown, navy, red, and green
- Scissors—one small pair and one pair of fabric shears
- Cloth measuring tape
- Pincushion with straight pins
- Box of safety pins
- Sewing needles in various sizes
- Thimble
- Box of assorted buttons
- Seam ripper
- Fabric marker

TACKLE BOX

Tackle boxes meant for fishing provide dozens of compartments perfect for spare buttons, safety pins, extra zippers, sequins, thimbles, threaders, etc. In the main compartment, there's plenty of room for larger tools, pincushions, and spools of thread.

204 Stocking a household emergency kit

When preparing an emergency kit, consider your family's food, water, light, and shelter needs, taking into account your local climate and geography. Emergency kit necessities include:

- Three-day supply of nonperishable food such as high-energy snacks, grains, and canned food. Consider pet and baby needs if applicable.
- Three-day water supply for each family member. Plan one gallon of water per person per day.
- Water purification tablets or unscented liquid bleach. (Sixteen drops will purify a gallon of water. Let it stand for thirty minutes before use.)
- Hand-cranked flashlights, which don't require batteries
- Battery-operated or hand-cranked radio
- Landline phone, which doesn't require power
- First aid kit (See entry 142, "First aid essentials.")
- Whistle, to signal for help
- Multifunction pocketknife including can opener and scissors
- Dust masks
- Plastic sheeting and duct tape
- Moist towelettes and plastic bags for personal hygiene and sanitation
- Cash in small denominations
- Copies of important documents in a waterproof pouch

205 How to maintain the linen closet

- Assign shelves to different types of linens—bed, bath, and table. Further organize by room (master bedroom, master bath, kids' bedrooms, kids' bath, guest bed and bath).
- Label shelf edges to keep piles in order.
- Use shelf dividers or linen organizers to keep stacks from toppling over. Piles of washcloths and hand towels are especially precarious.
- Store out-of-season linens (beach towels in winter, flannel sheets in summer) on the back of shelves or higher up.
- Use bins or baskets to contain toiletries and cleaning supplies.

206 Antique quilt storage

The best way to store an antique quilt is to spread it on a spare bed. For added protection, cover it with an everyday bed cover. Avoid direct sunlight as well as high-wattage, heat-producing lightbulbs. If you must fold a quilt for storage, lay the quilt facedown in between two well-worn cotton sheets, fold it in thirds and then roll to store. The idea is to minimize the stress on the fabric at the folds. Store quilts in plastic bins but never wrap them in plastic. Avoid contact with wood or paper products, whose acidity can cause quilt fibers to deteriorate. This includes cardboard boxes and even acid-free paper, which loses its coating over time. Remove and refold quilts every three to six months and air them out every six months.

207 Storing fine art

Framed. Cover individually in wrap with air pockets and store in frame boxes (cardboard boxes used for moving pictures and mirrors). Store upright in a cool, dry place.

Unframed. Lay flat in acid-free archival flat-storage boxes. Separate each piece with acid- and lignin-free archival tissue paper. To keep art from warping or cracking, keep boxes in a cool, dry place.

208 Vase basics

Pare your collection to the essentials; bud vases (to hold a single stem), globe-shaped vases (to hold a bunch of short-stemmed flowers), and cylindrical vases (for long-stemmed bouquets). Keep only as many vases as you will use at one time. If space is short, nest vases inside one another using air-filled wrap or paper towels in between to prevent breakage. Store vases out of the way on a high shelf until needed.

209 Gift wrap and ribbon

Take a twenty-four-pocket overdoor shoe organizer and hang it on the inside of a linen or utility closet. There will be four pockets across and six pockets down. Distribute wrapping materials such as gift tags, stickers, ribbon, bows, tape, and scissors into the compartments. To accommodate tubes of wrapping paper, cut holes in the upper compartments and thread the tube through the openings, letting it rest in the lower compartment.

210 Holiday decorations

Having decorations organized makes holiday entertaining less stressful. Use large plastic stackable bins to hold decorations for each holiday. Label them accordingly (Halloween, Thanksgiving, Xmas,

Hanukkah) and stack boxes with the labels facing out in the garage, basement, or attic. If there is more than one box per holiday, be sure to be specific on the label so you don't have to open multiple boxes to find what you are looking for.

Wreaths. To prevent crushing, store in a wreath box or wrap in a large plastic garbage bag and hang on a wall in the garage, attic, or basement (with a nail under the top and bottom to retain the wreath's shape).

Light strings. Take an empty wrapping paper tube and cut it in half. Wind the lights around the tube. Cut a slit in either end of the tube and stick the ends of the light strings in the slit to prevent the lights from unraveling. Use a piece of masking tape to label one end of the tube and specify where the lights go (tree, mantel, along the roof, etc.) to save you the effort of having to figure it out each season.

Ornaments. Protect delicate ornaments in padded ornament boxes with dividers to prevent them from bumping up against one another. Use shredded paper in each compartment to keep ornaments in place. Wrap extra-fragile ornaments in tissue paper and use a resealable plastic sandwich bag for ornaments made with glitter or dough.

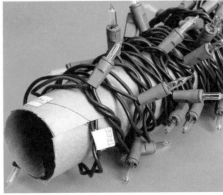

211 The organized garage

Keep two principles in mind: visibility and access. Arrange items so that you can see everything you have and store things according to how frequently you need them. To maximize space, utilize the walls and ceiling. Four tools will help you achieve this:

1. **Shelves and plastic storage bins.** Store seasonal sports equipment, holiday decorations, camping equipment, out-of-season clothing, ski and snowboarding gear, and bulky tools in large plastic bins. Stackable plastic drawers are a great way to manage household supplies such as lightbulbs, vacuum cleaner bags, and batteries. Use a large font on your label maker to clearly ID boxes.

2. **Garage storage wall system.** Make use of wall space with a garage storage wall system. Peg-Board is one option. Hooks can be positioned as desired to hold tools, rakes, brooms, garden hoses, beach chairs, etc. Several companies manufacture wall panel systems, complete with hooks, shelves, and storage cabinets that allow you to store the heaviest of objects, such as a bicycle, wheelbarrow, circular saw, and ladder.

3. **Ceiling storage.** A number of overhead storage systems on the market suspend from the ceiling or rafters and can hold up to a thousand pounds. Smaller versions are available that are perfect for out-of-season gear like snowboards and cross-country skis in the summer and surfboards and boogie boards in the winter.

4. **Workbench.** Whatever your passion—gardening, home improvement, or tinkering with the car—a workbench can help keep you organized and also provide a work and storage space. A Peg-Board above a workbench is ideal for hanging tools. (See entry 213, "How to organize tools.") Shelving can hold garden pots and soil or clear stacked plastic shoe boxes for home improvement items like sandpaper, Spackle, caulk, rope, tape, and gloves.

Keep everything off the floor to make it easy to sweep and clean. Applying epoxy paint to the floor of the garage will eliminate dust produced by porous concrete. Choose a color such as a medium gray that will show the least amount of dirt while still reflecting light. Prep floors thoroughly prior to painting according to instructions on the paint can.

212 The virtual garage sale

Use the power of the Internet to help rid your home of unwanted stuff and earn a little spending money. If you want to sell locally (meaning buyers can pick up your items), two sites that don't charge a listing or sales fee are craigslist.org and buysellcommunity.com. To reach a larger audience (and if you don't mind shipping items), try Amazon or eBay. A few things to keep in mind:

- List sole items only if they are worth the effort of shipping individually.
- Create a clear, concise heading that draws attention to the salient details of the item. Be honest in your description.
- Include clear photos.
- Find out what similar items sell for and set your sale price slightly lower. For eBay's listings, decide what the minimum amount you'd accept is, and make this your reserve amount. However, start the bidding low to attract interest.
- Amazon listings are free, but Amazon takes its cut before dispersing the rest to you. EBay charges a small insertion fee plus a final value fee if your listing sells.
- For local pickups, accept only cash and make this clear in your ad.

213 How to organize tools

Collect all your tools, putting aside duplicates or ones that you simply don't use, including anything rusty or broken. Donate the useable ones to a local Goodwill or Salvation Army. Consider the rest and decide on the appropriate size toolbox for your needs. For larger and bulky tools, hang Peg-Board on a wall in the garage. (You can screw right through the board into studs on the wall.) Arrange hooks to accommodate your tools. If you don't plan on moving tools around, you can trace the shape of each tool with an indelible ink marker so that you'll know where to put each one back when you take several down at once. An indispensable accessory for a toolbox or workbench is a plastic storage box or utility chest with multiple compartments to contain and organize all those little spare parts such as nails, screws, nuts, bolts, washers, anchors, and picture hooks.

QUICK TIP: **Cord Holder**

For an inexpensive solution to keeping extension cords neat and untangled, wind them tightly and store them in cardboard toilet paper tubes. This works for every spare electrical cord you need to store.

214 Ten essential toolbox items

1. Hammer. Choose one weighing 16 to 22 ounces, depending on what is comfortable to grip.

2. Screwdrivers. At least three sizes of both regular and Phillips head.

3. Pliers. Locking pliers with a two-inch jaw opening. Needle-nose pliers and a wire cutter are good to have too.

4. Wrench. Adjustable.

5. Tape measure. Twenty-five feet.

6. Drill and drill bit set. Go cordless for convenience, although you'll spend more money up front.

7. Level. A twelve-inch one is sufficient for basic hanging jobs.

8. Saw. A basic twenty-two-inch ten-to-twelve-tooth crosscut handsaw should do.

9. Utility knife and extra blades. Choose one with a retractable blade for safety.

10. Stud finder. Helpful for hanging pictures, shelves, or anything else on the walls.

Other items that will come in handy for general home improvement and repair tasks are: string, duct tape, nails and screws in various sizes, canvas or leather gloves, a pencil, super glue, Spackle, twelve-inch ruler, Velcro, scissors, cup hooks, and picture hooks and wire.

TOOL BUCKETS

A tool bucket makes it easy to carry whatever you need for do-it-yourself and fix-it projects around the house. Convert any standard five-gallon bucket into a mobile open-top toolbox with a multipocket bucket tool organizer. Put frequently used tools in the outer pockets and reserve the spacious interior for toting bulkier tools such as a drill and accessories.

215 Keeping paint for future touch-ups

The key to storing paint for future use is to keep air out of the can. Use these strategies:

- **Clean the rim.** Getting paint off the lip of the can creates an airtight seal.
- **Layer.** Place a piece of plastic wrap between the can and lid to ensure a tight seal.
- **Close firmly.** Lay a piece of wood on top of the lid and tap it with a hammer all the way around. Never hammer the lid directly as it will warp the lid and prevent a proper seal.
- **Label.** Write on the side of the can with a permanent marker: brand, shade, color code, where it was used (e.g., living room trim), and the date purchased.
- **Store.** If sealing with plastic, store cans upright. Some suggest storing paint cans upside down so the thin paint skin forms on the bottom. Storing them upright, however, you can remove the top skin so that it doesn't get mixed into the paint. Store cans in a cool place, avoiding extreme heat and freezing temperatures, such as the garage, which will ruin paint.

216 Do a home inventory

Keeping an up-to-date home inventory can help you purchase accurate insurance coverage and expedite claims in the event of theft or natural disaster. An inventory also comes in handy when making a will or renting out your house. Three options:

1. **Photograph.** Take digital photographs and print several on a sheet of photo paper. Adhere mailing labels to the back and write the salient information such as make and model, date, place of purchase, and price paid.

2. **Videotape.** Walk through your house with a video camera filming what you own and speak the relevant information as you go. Store photos and videos outside the home in a safe deposit box or with a friend.

3. **Home inventory software.** The Insurance Information Institute offers free home inventory software, which enables you to organize your inventory by room or category (furniture, electronics, appliances, furnishings, etc.). You can upload photos, receipts, appraisals, and easily update it when you purchase something new. The Web site (www.knowyourstuff.org) stores your inventory record online. Keep in mind that big-ticket items such as art, jewelry, and collectibles may require a separate policy.

217   Safe basement storage

If your basement tends to be damp, avoid storing items subject to mold, mildew, or rust such as anything made of fabric, paper, or metal. If you do need to store such vulnerable articles, put them in sealable plastic bags inside plastic bins and add silica gel packets to absorb moisture. Elevate valuable items and chemicals (including paint) in case of flooding. As a general rule, choose metal shelving instead of wood and plastic boxes instead of cardboard. Keep the area around the water heater and furnace clear. Having adequate lighting in the basement will help you not only locate what you are looking for but also help you spot any signs of mold and mildew growth.

218   Basement shelving

Shelving can significantly expand storage capacity in the basement. Sturdy, adjustable metal shelving such as Metro Shelving is a good bet for long-term basement storage. Look for easy-to-assemble units that allow you to choose and adjust shelf height. Figure out what you need to store, organize it into plastic storage containers where appropriate, and then space shelves according to your storage needs, remembering that the heaviest items go on the bottom shelf.

QUICK TIP: **Dividers**

Make use of unused vertical space and triple or quadruple storage capacity by dividing the garage with a row of stand-alone shelving in between cars.

utility and storage areas

219 Protect yard furniture during winter months

To make your summer furniture last longer, follow these steps before putting it away for the season:

- Pillows. Completely dry before storing. Store in ventilated plastic boxes. (Cut holes in the plastic boxes with a knife or scissors to provide ventilation.)
- Table umbrellas. Wash with mild soap in cold water with a soft bristled brush. Dry completely. Oil frame joints at the start of each new season.
- Fabric chair covers. Machine wash according to manufacturer instructions (usually on gentle cycle). Line dry and put back on the chair while still slightly damp to protect against shrinkage.
- Plastic, wood, and wicker sets. Clean with mild soap and water and stack if possible.

QUICK TIP: **Outside Protection**

If you don't have space to store outdoor furniture inside, invest in a set of all-weather covers to protect furnishings from the winter elements. Look for Velcro bands or drawstring cords that hold covers tightly in place. Clean furniture according to manufacturer instructions and dry completely before covering.

what's a disorganized person to do?

220 Winterize your lawn mower

After the leaves have come down, but before the first snow, follow these procedures to ensure your lawn mower's long life:

Gas mower

1. **Tend to the gas tank.** Run it outside to use up the remaining gas or siphon it out.

2. **Change the oil.** Drain out the old and replace with new lawnmower motor oil. Be sure to dispose of the old oil correctly, either at a recycling center or your local service center. (See entry 33, "Recycling resources.")

3. **Check spark plug for corrosion.** Replace if necessary. Pour an ounce of oil into the cylinders, replace the spark plug, and crank the engine a few times to distribute the oil.

4. **Clean or replace the air filter.** Soak spongy filters in warm soapy water, rinse, and let air dry. Then lightly coat the filter with a tablespoon of clean motor oil.

5. **Charge the battery.** Most lawnmowers don't charge the battery completely while running. Doing so now and a few times during the season will help the battery hold its charge.

For all mowers

1. **Clean the mower.** Use a tool to remove grass clippings, mud, and other debris from the blades and underside of the housing. Hose off the rest and dry thoroughly.

2. **Sharpen the blade.** Professionally sharpen the blade annually.

3. **Check the tires.** If they take air, keeping sufficient air pressure in the tires makes the machine easier to roll.

4. **Store in a cool, dry place.** Cover with cloth rather than plastic, as plastic can trap in moisture.

utility and storage areas

221 Prepare your grill for hibernation

Take a few steps at the end of the season to ensure that your grill is ready to go at the first sign of spring:

1. **Clean thoroughly.** If possible, take the grill apart and scrape burners and grates with a wire brush to get rid of built-up grease and food. Rinse out the shell with warm soapy water. Dry completely before reassembling. For a gas grill, start it up and run for ten to fifteen minutes to make sure all parts are completely dry.

2. **Check manufacturer instructions.** If a protective coat of oil is recommended, lightly cover all metal parts with cooking oil to prevent rust.

3. **Detach propane tanks.** Choose a well-ventilated area protected from weather and elevate the tank off the ground on a flat, nonburnable base, storing upright for safety. *Do not store in the garage or basement* because propane is highly explosive, and propane gas fires are extremely destructive. A detached shed away from the house is ideal for storing tanks.

4. **Store the grill indoors.** Otherwise, choose a place outside, preferably under an overhang, where it will be sheltered from rain and snow. Invest in a waterproof cover to keep dirt and moisture out.

Properly stacking firewood helps logs stay dry and keeps the pile stable. Choose a flat, even spot of ground and lay wooden shipping pallets so that firewood sits a good three inches above the ground to keep wood clean, bug-free, and, most important, dry. To create a stable base, begin stacking the flattest (hence, most stable) pieces along the front of the pallet with ends facing out. Lay each new row so that it crisscrosses the one beneath it. Arrange logs so that they tip in toward the center of the pile, taking the weight of the wood inward rather than out, and leave a bit of space between logs for air to circulate. For safety, limit the height of the pile to four feet. Cover the pile with a tarp to keep it dry. The tarp should be free of holes and large enough to cover the pile and drape on the ground around it an additional couple of feet. Anchor the tarp on the top of the pile with stones and tie the bottom of the tarp to the pallets.

QUICK TIP: **Silica Packets**

Reuse silica gel packets by putting them in the oven on a low temperature for about twenty minutes. This will remove any moisture that they've absorbed. Let the packet cool before you reuse it.

utility and storage areas

223 Organizing sports equipment

Who knows, you might just be a bit more active if you can actually find the athletic gear you want:

- Hang mesh bags from hooks to hold tennis, golf, and baseballs. Mount wire baskets on a wall for soccer balls, basketballs, and volleyballs.
- Store long items such as hockey and lacrosse sticks, baseball bats, racquets, and golf clubs upright in tall cylindrical containers. Try an umbrella stand or a garbage can and weight the bottom if necessary.
- Use a system of open plastic bins on shelves for miscellaneous gear. Keep items that are used together in the same bin and label accordingly. For instance, store knee and elbow pads, wrist guards, helmets, and skate totes in one bin; beach gear such as shovels, pails, beach balls, and a Frisbee in another. Then just load the whole bin into the trunk of your car and be ready to go.
- Install wall-mounted racks to get larger items up off the floor. A simple rack system with hooks can hold almost all your outdoor gear like bicycles, skis, snowboards, surfboards, skateboards, sleds, ice skates, and in-line skates.

224 Make the most of storage space

A well-organized storage shed or attic can help eliminate household clutter, but should contain only items that have present or future utility. Good organization is essential, especially
for accessing what you need when
you need it.

- **Clean.** If you are reorganizing a space you currently have, sweep the floors, mop up spills, and wipe down walls and corners to get rid of cobwebs and
critters. Lay down a floor cover to further protect your belongings.
- **Inventory.** As you store items, inventory furniture and appliances as well as the number of boxes and their contents.
- **Label.** Label boxes on all sides. Be specific to quickly ID what you need.
- **Load.** Load large furniture items and appliances in first, against the back wall. Leave at least an inch of space between the wall and your stored items to allow air to circulate. Cover these items with furniture covers or plastic to protect them from dust and other potential damage.
- **Stack.** Same-sized boxes stack best and are easiest to restack if you need something at the bottom. If you plan to frequently access boxes, or if boxes hold fragile items and can't be stacked, invest in an inexpensive shelving unit. Make sure shelves are deep and wide enough to accommodate your boxes.

Reining It In
Kid Clutter

While some people seem to have been born with an organizing gene, the vast majority of us need to acquire the habit. While children love to make messes, cleanup can also be fun. What's more, kids thrive on order. Now is the time to instill good habits, which your little ones will keep for a lifetime.

225 The ABCs of organization

Even very young children can be taught to put things away in their proper place. Use these strategies:

Ask kids for help. Work with young children to help them to put things away until it becomes a habit. Toddlers will take pride in their ability to be helpful. For older kids, positive reinforcement methods such as an allowance can make this kind of maintenance part of their daily duties.

Books with books. Teach kids to group items in categories: toys with toys, games with games, dolls with dolls, and crayons with crayons.

Create a place for everything. Teach your kids that everything they own—toys, books, clothing, and everything else—has a home, just like they do. And at the end of the day, all things return to their home.

226 Hooked on hooks

Hooks are a simple yet effective organization tool for kids. Hooks hung at an accessible level in or near the entryway make it easy for kids to hang up (and later locate) things like hats, coats, scarves, and backpacks. Use hooks in the bathroom to keep towels off the floor and hooks in a bedroom closet for favorite hard-to-fold items like sweatshirts and bathrobes.

227   Hand-me-downs

If age gaps between kids are small, consider storing hand-me-downs in the receiving child's closet on a high shelf. If age gaps between kids are larger, and longer-term storage is required, then store clothing in labeled plastic bins with secure lids in the garage, attic, basement, or any other cool and dry storage area within the house. Make sure the clothing is clean and dry when you store it, as stains and dampness will attract bugs and mildew. Organize the clothing by age and size and, if needed, by season, and label the outside of boxes clearly (with age/size/season). That way, when a child comes of age, you will only have to pull one box at a time. If you have to store clothing in the basement or anywhere potentially damp, add packets of silica gel to the boxes to absorb moisture. (See entry 217, "Safe basement storage.") Maternity clothes can be stored in the same way, labeling boxes with the trimester and season.

228   How to get kids to use the hamper

Easy access is the smartest bet for getting your kids to put their dirty clothes in a hamper. Out of sight will probably mean out of mind. An open hamper or a laundry basket (one that doesn't require lifting a lid) on the floor will have increased chances of being used and is the best option for toddlers and young children. Or keep a hamper near the bathroom, where they take off their clothes. For older kids, hang a basketball hoop over the hamper so kids will feel inspired to take aim, shoot, and, hopefully, score.

229 Kid-friendly closets

When designing a closet, keep adaptability for growing kids in mind.

1. Opt for adjustable drawers, rods, and shelves that can be repositioned as your child grows.

2. Make access easy. Place the most often worn and used things within a child's reach.

3. Use higher rods and shelves for out-of-season clothing or less frequently worn items.

4. Sliding baskets are great for t-shirts, pajamas, socks, and underwear since kids can see what's inside, and baskets are easy to slide open.

5. Keep shoes off the floor with shoe cubbies, containers, or canvas shoe storage that hangs from the rod.

6. For small children, open bins on the floor of the closet are the most user-friendly—and therefore successful—storage solution.

QUICK TIP: **Outfits in Advance**

Get your kids out the door on time by laying out their clothes for the upcoming week. Use a six-compartment hanging sweater bag to organize outfits by day, labeling each shelf with the days of the school week. Use the bottom shelf for shoes or other accessories.

230 A kid's-eye view

Adopt the activity-centered model of a kindergarten classroom to organize your child's room. Have an area for reading, an area for crafts, an area for dress-up. Get down low to see the room from a child's perspective and organize from the bottom of the room upward. Store most frequently used toys where kids can reach them—on bottom shelves, in lower drawers, and in a toy chest or other containers on the floor. Toys and games that require adult participation or supervision should be stored on higher shelves.

QUICK TIP: **Toy Wrangling**

Place baskets strategically around the house to help corral migrating toys and get them back to their assigned home. If you live in a multistoried home, choose one that fits on a stair and can serve as a halfway house, encouraging kids to pick up their toys, put them in one place, and take them upstairs later (works for grown-ups too).

---

231 When to toss: toys

Toss toys that are broken, worn out, or unsafe. But donate toys that are in good condition if your kids have outgrown, never liked, or no longer play with them. Go through toys at least every six months or before birthdays and holidays to make room for new playthings. Instill a sense of philanthropy in your young ones by helping them choose a charity to which they can donate their toys.

232 The naming game

stuffed animals

blocks

musical instruments

For kids who can't yet read, create labels by printing images off the computer. Do a Google search for each category (stuffed animals, cars and trucks, dolls, etc.), and click on Images to find a picture for your label. Pull the picture into a Word document, write the category name below the image, and size it according to how big you want the label. Print, cut to size, and laminate the photo using self-sealing laminating sheets (which work without heat or special tools). Punch a hole at the top, thread a piece of string or ribbon through it, and tie it to the respective basket, bucket, or bin. For plastic bins without a handle, try printing images on adhesive-backed paper and adhere the labels directly onto the plastic.

QUICK TIP: **Fight Boredom**

Kids get bored with toys so quickly and can even be overwhelmed by too many choices. So if toys are taking over your house, limit the number of toys in rotation at any one time to what comfortably fits in storage areas you've allotted. Store excess toys in clear plastic bins in an out-of-the-way place, and every month or so, rotate new ones out. Kids will get excited all over again at their new selection of toys.

233 Fun and games

Toys are the biggest source of kid room clutter. A variety of toy storage solutions works best as children's toy collections grow.

1. Keep books on low sturdy shelves where they are accessible. For toddlers, books in a basket or two on a low shelf let kids pull the basket off the shelf and flip through books to find what they want. Then the book can be put back in the front of the basket when reading is done.

2. Stack game boxes on shelves stored in mesh cubes. Keep small game pieces in sandwich-bags to avoid losing them. Encourage kids to play with one game at a time and put one away before taking another one out, so that pieces don't mix and match.

3. Store large toys such as musical instruments and trucks in a toy chest or large collapsible mesh bins.

4. Sort small toys into categories such as blocks, action figures, and dolls, and store them in easy-to-handle bins or baskets on shelves.

5. Use stackable clear plastic boxes with lids to contain small pieces like LEGOS, Barbie accessories, and army men. Label accordingly and stack them on shelves.

6. Assign a special shelf for kids to display their collections, whether it be rocks, shells, fairies, trolls, trains, baseballs, etc. Collect small items in a large clear jar so that they are visible, but contained.

7. What about all the tiny things kids accumulate such as cereal box toys, party favors, and souvenirs? Hang an overdoor shoe organizer with clear vinyl pockets on the back of their bedroom or closet door. Rotate things they don't use as often to higher pockets and eventually out as more space is needed.

8. Plastic boxes with handles let kids tote art supplies to work stations.

234 Stuffed animal overload

If your young stuffed animal aficionado has made it clear that population control is out of the question, try the following strategies for keeping furry friends corralled.

- Toy hammock. Hang it in a corner of the bedroom, low enough for your child to reach. Mesh netting can also serve the same purpose.
- Overdoor multipocket shoe organizer. For small stuffed animals, hang an overdoor shoe organizer on the back of a closet or bedroom door and stick a stuffed animal (or two) in each pocket.
- Toy box. A shallow toy box on the floor makes for easy access without too much digging and also facilitates easy cleanup.

QUICK TIP: **Traveling with Baby**

NEVER travel by airplane without packing in your carry-on a change of clothes for you, your baby, your spouse, and any other family members. There is nothing worse than getting thrown up on and having to wear it for the rest of the flight!

235   Diaper bag do's

The key is to know your child and to anticipate his or her possible needs. While it's important to be prepared, you don't want to lug around too much weight. Do pack:

• Diapers. At least three to five, and more for longer journeys.
• Travel wipes.
• Changing pad.
• Burp cloths.
• Diaper cream. Dispense some into a small travel-size container and leave the tube at home.
• Diaper bags.
• Entertainment. Depending on age, books and/or a toy.
• Snacks. For baby, and also for Mom!
• Hat. Depending on the season, a winter hat or a sun hat.
• Extra outfit. Keep it light, since it's just backup.
• Baby water bottle or sippy cup.

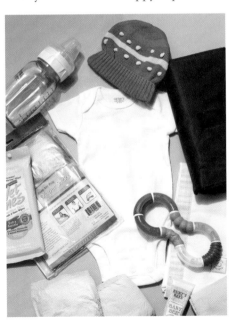

236 Six strategies for children's artwork

Young budding Picassos can produce a prodigious amount of artwork. Here's how to decide what to save, and how to display and store the keepers. Create a special area (other than the fridge!) to display your child's best works. To limit the number of works on display, keep art in constant rotation. Some options:

1. **Wall-mounted cable system.** Stainless-steel cable with clips for hanging shower curtains or window panels can also display rotating artwork. For a cheaper alternative, use a clothesline and clothespins or picture wire with binder clips.

2. **Frames.** Frame select works and designate a wall or hallway to serve as a gallery. Rotate art through the frames.

3. **Homasote.** An environmentally friendly dartboardlike tack board, Homasote is great for displaying artwork and other memorabilia. Available at hardware stores in four-by-eight-foot panels, Homasote can be cut to size. Cover the panel(s) with a fabric of your choosing and use pushpins to hang art and anything else.

4. **Magnetize a wall.** Apply at least four coats of magnetic wall paint primer (such as Magic Wall, which is available at hardware outlets and some toy stores) and then paint your desired color over it. Use extra-strength magnets to hold up artwork, as regular fridge magnets aren't strong enough.

5. Share the love. Give to Grandma. Since even *she* can accommodate only so much, send some to friends and other relatives (who won't feel as attached and can eventually purge with greater abandon).

6. Gift wrap. If your child can handle his or her artwork being ripped apart, use it to wrap presents. Tape a few together for larger gifts.

237 What artwork is worth keeping?

Let children help decide what to save. What a parent often sees as a scribble can be a very important work for a child and should be honored, says New York City kindergarten teacher Victoria Misrock Stein. A collection of a child's work should reflect that child over time, so it doesn't have to be just their best work. Save a drawing (or two) from each month and make sure the work is dated.

238 Go digital

Immortalize your child's artwork with technology:

- Create a Flickr account. Take digital images of your child's artwork and upload them to Flickr (www.flickr.com). Send the link to grandparents, godparents, and anyone else who might be interested.
- Scan art. Scan pieces of artwork or take digital photos and upload to any image hosting/photo sharing Web site such as Snapfish or Kodak Gallery. You can even create mugs, puzzles, tote bags, T-shirts, stamps, or pillowcases memorializing your child's art.

- **Make a coffee table book.** You can do this through either of the above-mentioned Web sites, Blurb, or iPhoto. This is a great solution for 3-D art that is unwieldy and hard to store. Most services will allow you to add captions so that you can record the title of the piece, your child's age, the date, and any other pertinent details.

239 How to store artwork

Because of the volume of art that kids produce, saving your child's artwork should be a continual selection and editing process. Short-term storage means having both a display area and a holding area. Collect art that you might want to save, but aren't displaying, in a temporary holding bin (such as a tray, basket, or box on a counter or shelf). Once a month, go through the box with your child and choose one or two pieces that are worth keeping. Store the keepers in a large art portfolio (the brown oak-tag portfolios with handles are great). Inside, separate the child's work by year. Take an easel-size piece of paper and fold it in half. Keep one year at a time inside that sleeve and date the sleeve. (For example, KINDERGARTEN, AGE 5, 2008.) If the work is 3-D, you can either photograph it and save a digital image of it or display one or two important pieces as part of a permanent sculpture collection in the house.

240 "Where's my backpack?"

Three words you never want to hear, especially on your way out the door. Kids should have an assigned place for their backpacks, somewhere in or near the entryway where it is convenient for them to unload important papers and homework assignments after a day at school and where parents can easily repack things they'll need for the following day. An entryway cubby system with one cubby for each kid is a great way to assign and delineate space. Hang a wall sorter to capture school papers such as homework assignments and notes from teachers. This prevents paper from accumulating on kitchen counters. Choose one day a week to sort through and clean out backpacks.

241 Welcome home: rules for reentry

Teach kids to hang their coats on pegs, take off their shoes, and unload their backpacks when they return home. Train them to empty their lunch boxes, leaving them in an appointed spot, and to put their folder of school papers in a designated in-box on the counter. As they get older, increase their responsibilities, having them separate their artwork, homework, and school papers and put them in their respective places (artwork on a tray or in a bin, homework on their desk, and school papers in Mom's in-box).

242 Sorting school papers

Short-term
Set up a filing system in the kitchen for current school papers, or keep papers in a binder with tabbed dividers. Try a clear acrylic magnetic file holder or wall file sorter on the side of the refrigerator or inside a pantry door. Set up four files inside:

1. Contact lists. School contact numbers and classroom and team rosters.

2. Schedules. School, sports, and afterschool activity schedules. (But first transfer dates to a master family calendar.)

3. Current papers. All school announcements, including events, field trip information, fund-raisers, and newsletters. (Use one file for each child.) Purge this folder frequently.

4. To-do. Forms to fill out, book orders, and anything requiring action.

When kids get home from school, treat their papers like mail, first sorting what's important from the junk, which gets thrown out. Important papers go straight from backpacks into the appropriate folders. The "to-do" folder is reviewed daily, and current papers are sorted through weekly. Use a magnetic bulldog clip on the fridge to hold immediate "to-do" items like permission slips.

Long-term
Keep only what is truly important: report cards, awards, acknowledgments, and special projects. For each child, use a large (three-inch) binder. Label the spine with the child's name. Delineate school years with dividers. Three-hole punch important papers and insert them into the binder.

243 Keeping track of schedules

Use one master calendar. Designate one parent the Schedule Master. For a stay-at-home Schedule Master, a calendar in the kitchen with large squares can serve as a master calendar and communication device so that spouses and other caretakers stay informed about who's going where. A day planner or PDA is probably better for Schedule Masters on the go. Shared digital calendars are the best for communicating ever-changing complex schedules between busy partners. Rapidly changing technology makes having a virtual up-to-the-minute exchange of data increasingly easier. Whatever your technology, when your child comes home from school with papers galore, transfer important dates to the calendar ASAP. Include school events, field trips, holidays, playdates, doctor appointments, lessons, sports schedules, etc. If you are using a shared digital calendar, color-code appointments to show who does the carpooling.

244 Time capsules

Give children a box in which to save their childhood memorabilia. Then label it and let them keep it in their closet. Contents of the box should reflect milestones, achievements, and memorable experiences such as his or her birth announcement, a lock of hair, first pair of baby shoes, first lost tooth, first-place ribbons, ticket stub to first concert, junior prom invitation, etc. If the box fills up, start another and label the first box with the appropriate years.

kid clutter

On the Go
From Trips to Moves

Whether you are changing handbags or houses, flying to Boston or Beijing, carpooling or driving across the country, being organized when you're on the move will help keep you sane. From securing your home when you're on vacation to packing just enough (and not more) for a trip, the following tips will help you stay in control wherever you go.

245 Handbag how-to

Handbags are often a microcosm of one's life in general. The same rules of organization still apply:

- **Keep like things together.** Use small zippered bags to contain such items as makeup. This makes it easier to move items when changing handbags, as well.
- **Give everything a home.** Choose a handbag with pockets and designate one for sunglasses, one for keys, and one for your cell phone. Assign a place in your wallet to keep receipts, another for store credits and gift certificates.
- **Put things back.** Rather than haphazardly tossing things into your handbag, take an extra minute to put cash or change in your wallet, receipts in their designated place, or a colleague's business card in your planner or notebook. Aim to have nothing floating at the bottom of your bag except larger items like your wallet, eyeglass case, or planner.

246 In brief

A briefcase is essentially your portable office, so you need a place for files, supplies, and equipment.

- **Files.** Rather than stuffing all needed papers into an undifferentiated file, divide them according to projects or clients, subdividing further as needed. Keep the most important files in the front and reading materials or reference papers toward the back.
- **Supplies.** Use interior pockets for pens, sticky notes, paper clips, and a notepad.
- **Equipment.** Designate other inside pockets for mobile phone, glasses, keys, etc. Check these places before you leave to ensure you haven't forgotten anything.

247 Prepare for departure

Before leaving your home for an extended period:

- Arrange for care of plants, pets, yard, and mail.
- Pay bills in advance.
- Empty perishables from fridge.
- Take out the trash.
- Unplug appliances and electronics.
- Close fireplace flue.
- Lock doors and windows.
- Set thermostat to a reasonable level for pets and plants left behind.
- Make sure stove and oven are turned off.
- Store valuables in a safe place.
- Leave a key and itinerary with a neighbor.
- Leave some lights on or set timers to deter burglars. Set timers for TVs too.
- Cancel newspaper delivery. Piled-up papers signal that nobody is home.
- Ask a neighbor to collect any flyers or circulars left on your driveway or doorstep and to put the trash cans out on pickup day.

248 What to pack

A packing list should ensure that you don't forget anything important while preventing you from packing too much. Start by creating an exhaustive list of all the things you might need on a trip, including clothing, cosmetics, gear, documents, and specialty items. Since the type of trip you are taking will dictate what you bring, the list serves as a checklist and not a packing list. After each trip, refine your list by deleting extraneous items and adding what would have benefited you.

Consider creating separate lists for specific types of trips that require vastly different items. For instance, you might make one list for business trips and another for camping.

249 Sample packing lists

Clothing Essentials

For everybody
Flip-flops
Jacket
Pajamas
Shirts
Shorts
Socks
Sweaters or sweatshirts
Trousers and/or pants
T-shirts
Underwear
Walking shoes

Kids
Sandals
Sneakers

Men
Belt
Dressy shoes
Workout clothes

Women
Belt
Bras
Dresses
Dressy shoes
Sandals
Workout clothes

First Aid

Antibiotic
Bandages
Cold medicine
Diarrhea remedy
First aid kit
Hand sanitizer or wipes
Hydrocortisone cream

Insect repellent
Motion sickness remedy
Pain relievers
Prescription medications
Triple antibiotic ointment
Vitamins & supplements

Gadgets

Batteries
Camera & charger
Extra memory cards/film
GPS device
Laptop & power cord

MP3 player & charger
Portable DVD player
Smart/cell phone & charger
Video camera & charger

Important Documents

Cash
Contact info for credit cards
Credit & ATM cards
Driver's license
Health insurance info

Itineraries
Photocopies of important docs
Travel tickets & reservations
Travelers' checks

Personal Hygiene

Brush or comb
Clothes-washing soap packets
Contact lenses & solution
Cosmetics
Cotton swabs
Deodorant
Feminine hygiene products
Floss
Glasses
Moisturizer (face & body)

Nail clippers
Razor
Shampoo & conditioner
Shaving cream
Soap
Sunscreen & lip balm
Toothbrush
Toothpaste
Travel towel
Tweezers

from trips to moves

243

Travel Aids

Daypack

Earplugs

Flashlight

Luggage locks (TSA-approved)

Money belt

Reusable water bottle

Sewing kit

Swiss army knife*

Travel alarm clock

Travel blanket

Travel pillow

Umbrella

Pack in checked baggage

For any trip below, first consult the list of clothing essentials and add on using these lists:

Beach Vacation

Aloe (for sunburns)

Bathing suits

Beach chairs

Beach totes

Beach umbrella

Books

Cooler

Flip-flops or sandals

Frisbee and/or paddle ball

Mosquito net

Rash guards

Reusable water bottle

Sand toys (shovels, pails)

Sarong or beach cover-up

Sun hat

Sunglasses

Sunscreen

Surfboard or boogie board

Wetsuit

Business Trip

Belt

Briefcase

Dress socks or pantyhose

Dressy shoes

Laptop and case

Suit(s)

Ties or scarves

Watch

Camping Trip

Air mattress or sleeping pads
Can opener
Citronella candle & bug
    repellent
Clothesline
Compass and/or GPS
Cooking stove & fuel
Cooler
Dishes & cutlery
Extra drinking water
First aid kit
Handheld broom
    (to sweep tent)
Headlamp
Lantern
Lighter or matches
Mosquito net
Portable chairs or stools
Pots & pans
Shortwave radio
Sleeping bags
Tent & ground cover
Toilet paper & zip-top
    plastic bags
Water purification method

International Trip

Auto insurance card
Foreign currency
International student ID card
Passports and relevant visas
Phrase book or dictionary
SIM card
Universal electrical adapter
Vaccination records*
Water purification method

*Check with the Center for Disease Control (www.cdc.gov) for recommended
and/or required vaccinations for your destination.*

Ski Trip

After-ski boots
Après-sun lotion
Boots & carrying straps
Fanny pack
Gloves & liners
Goggles
Granola bars
Hand/toe warmers
Hat & earmuffs
Knee brace
Long underwear
Scarf or neck gator
Ski pants & jacket
Ski socks & liners
Ski sweaters
Skis & poles or snowboard
Sunglasses with neck strap
Sunscreen & lip balm

from trips to moves

Travel with Babies

Bibs

Bio-degradable diaper bags

Blanket

Bottles, caps & nipples

Burp cloths

Changing pad

Child-carrying sling

Diaper bag

Diaper cream

Disposable diapers

Hat

Portable high chair

Portable playpen

Room intercom

Snacks

Spoon

Stroller

Toys and/or books

Travel wipes

Travel with Kids

Books

Coloring books

Electronic games

Favorite pillow or blanket

Pens, crayons, pencils

Playing cards

Small games

Snacks

Stuffed animal or doll

Toys

Travel wipes

250 Dopp kit to go

Create a grab-and-go tote containing no more than three ounces each of your favorite self-care necessities. Decant products into plastic bottles and contain them in a zippered one-quart plastic bag. Pin a few safety pins to the hole in the zipper pull. (You never know when you'll need one.) Stash the bag in your favorite carry-on suitcase and be travel-ready at a moment's notice.

General

Toothpaste

Toothbrush

Floss

Deodorant

Body lotion

Hair styling products

Face cleanser

Face cream (for her)

Perfume samples (for her)

Shaving gel (for him)

251 Carry-on essentials

When it comes to your carry-on bag, pack only those items you will need during the flight or that you can't do without in the event that your checked luggage doesn't arrive. Your carry-on should include cash, jewelry, passport, travel documents (including itineraries), traveler's checks, keys, laptop and power cord, medications, makeup, toothpaste, toothbrush, and a clean pair of underwear.

from trips to moves

252 The travel essentials box

To keep from searching all over the house for small travel necessities, contain them in a large shoe or boot box. Label it and keep it somewhere accessible, especially if you travel frequently. It can contain:

- Passport
- Document organizer (for tickets, itineraries, etc.)
- Vaccination record
- Leftover foreign currency in labeled travel-ready envelopes (for example, EUROS or CANADIAN DOLLARS)
- Electrical adapters or a universal adapter
- A second set of power cords for laptop and cell phone
- Travel alarm
- Small flashlight
- Inflatable neck pillow
- Universal sink stopper (for washing clothes in the sink) and detergent packets
- Pocketknife (packed in your checked luggage, not a carry-on)
- Pocket-size foreign language pocket phrase books and dictionaries

Customize your box to suit your travel needs. When you return from a trip, unload these items back into the box for future travel.

253 How to travel light

- Create a travel wardrobe around one color—either black or brown.
- Lay out what you plan to pack and reduce what you think you need by half.
- Pack versatile basics that combine to create multiple outfits.
- Bring a few key accessories. (A bold tie or a vibrant scarf can take an outfit from day to night.)
- Depending on the type of trip you are taking, limit shoes to (at most) one pair of dressy, one pair for walking, and one pair of flip-flops or sandals.
- For cold-weather destinations, plan to layer rather than pack bulky sweaters, and wear your bulkiest items on the plane.
- When in doubt, leave it out.

QUICK TIP: **Traveling with Gifts**

Consider wrapping gifts when you arrive at your destination. In some cases, baggage inspectors will insist that you unwrap items for inspection.

254 What *not* to pack

- Blow dryer. Most hotels provide one. If you aren't sure, call ahead to ask.
- Toiletries. If you aren't too attached to your products, leave them home, since most hotels provide shampoo, conditioner, body lotion, and soap. If you do bring your own, reduce your beauty regimen down to essentials and bring small bottles. Find double-duty products such as moisturizer with SPF.
- Travel guides. Instead of carrying bulky guidebooks, visit Lonely

Planet (www.lonelyplanet.com), which lets you buy, download, and print chapters—à la carte style—to create your own guidebook covering only what's on your itinerary.

· Valuables. Unless you are attending a gala on your trip, leave valuable jewelry home. In places where tourists are targets for petty crime, expensive jewelry signals opportunity.

QUICK TIP: **Packing Cubes**

These lightweight microweave fabric cubes fit inside your suitcase and make it easy to find what you need without taking apart your entire bag. They come in various sizes. Use a small-size cube for socks, undergarments, and toiletries, and larger cubes for packing shirts, shorts, pants, and skirts. To conserve space and prevent wrinkling, roll garments instead of folding them.

---

255 What items are permitted in my carry-on?

Airport security measures are often changing, so for the most up-to-date list of approved carry-on items, check with the Transportation Security Administration (TSA) before you fly (www.tsa.gov). At the time of publication, the following items are allowed in the main cabin of the aircraft:

• Tweezers
• Nail clippers and nail files
• Eyelash curlers
• Safety razors (including disposable razors)

- Walking canes and umbrellas (inspected to ensure prohibited items are not concealed)
- Syringes (with accompanying medication and professionally printed labels identifying the medication or manufacturer)
- Insulin delivery systems
- Musical instruments (as long as they fit in your carry-on)
- Scissors with blades shorter than 4 inches
- Knitting needles are technically allowed but sometimes do get confiscated. Your best bet is to travel with bamboo or plastic needles (instead of metal) that are under 31 inches in length.
- Liquids, gels, and aerosols in 3-ounce (or smaller) containers. These must be kept in a 1-quart clear plastic zip-top bag. (TSA permits the following liquids to be carried on in reasonable quantities exceeding three ounces: medications, breast milk, baby formula, food, and juice).

The following items must be packed in checked baggage:

- Sporting equipment
- Sharp objects such as box cutters, ice picks, and knives (wrap them well to protect against injury)
- Disabling chemicals, including pepper spray
- Gel shoe inserts

Check with the TSA for a complete list of prohibited items:
www.tsa.gov/travelers/airtravel/prohibited/permitted-prohibited
-items.shtm

When working remotely, assign a specific ring tone for business contacts, clients, and your boss so you'll know when to turn down the music and answer your cell phone in your most businesslike demeanor.

256 How to work from anywhere

A laptop with wireless Internet capabilities and a smart cell phone (one that enables you to check your e-mail) is the starting point for a mobile office. Recommended add-ons include:

- A laptop connect card. This lets you gain wireless Internet access through your cell phone service if Wi-Fi is not available. (Costs are involved. Ask your cell phone provider for details.)
- File synchronization software. Changes made to a file at one location will show up at the other location when synchronized, thus keeping files at multiple workstations continually updated.
- Backup capabilities. Back up your computer to an external hard drive or do it online.
- File sharing capabilities. Depending on what kind of data needs to be shared with others, install project management, group chat, and document-sharing applications.

what's a disorganized person to do?

257 Traveling with technology

Frequent travel inspired me to invest in a second set of power cords for my laptop and cell phone. I keep these in my computer bag, ready to go when I am. When I upgraded my camera, I noticed that the cables connecting the camera to the computer for downloading were the same. So one stays in my desk drawer and the other in my travel box. It's the same story with the iPod. I keep an iPod charging dock in the travel box too, in case I travel without my computer. Keep all cords and chargers together in a bag inside the travel box so that all your technological devices are always ready to go. (See entry 252, "The travel essentials box.")

258 How to be a productive commuter

Don't just sit there, do something. Better yourself while you commute. Download free Harvard University (and other) courses from iTunes U (to your iPod or iPhone) or visit Open Culture (www.oculture.com) and download (in a variety of formats) courses ranging from existentialism to quantum entanglement. Or purchase a Great Courses lecture series on audio CD. Choose from 250 courses given by top university professors on a variety of topics.

QUICK TIP: **Suitcase Storage**

Nest suitcases to save space. Store travel-related accessories (such as shoe bags, neck pillows, duffle bags) inside suitcases. If storing suitcases in the basement or garage, cover them with a sheet or a laundry bag to protect them against dust.

from trips to moves

259 A well-stocked glove compartment

If your glove compartment is home to fast-food ketchup packets, service receipts, expired proofs of insurance, or other detritus, clean it out and restock it with the following items:

- Registration and proof of insurance (but not the title, which should be kept in a safe place at home)
- Owner's manual (demystify those flashing dashboard symbols)
- Small flashlight (instead of worrying about batteries, opt for a hand-cranked flashlight, which gives an hour of light per minute of cranking)
- Swiss army knife (you never know when you might need scissors, a can opener, or a screwdriver)
- Tire pressure gauge (correct tire pressure improves gas mileage and prolongs tire life)
- A cell phone charger
- Emergency contact (insurance agent, tow service, local police)
- Wet wipes (for sticky fingers, spills, or to wipe your hands after a visit to the pump)
- Pen and notebook (for recording information in case of an accident)

260 Your car's emergency kit

Every trunk should contain the following essentials:

Basics
• Flares or battery-powered warning light
• Weatherproof flashlight (that stands on its own for hands-free use)
• Extra fuses
• Jack and lug wrench for changing tires
• Jumper cables
• Extra quart of oil
• Fire extinguisher
• Help sign
• First aid kit (See entry 142, "First aid essentials.")
• Gloves and rags
• Disposable camera with a flash (to record damage for insurance
  purposes)

Long hauls
• Basic tool kit (Phillips and regular head screwdrivers, socket and
  open-end wrenches, pliers, electrical wire tape)
• Bottled drinking water
• Nonperishable emergency snacks
• GPS

Winter weather
• Folding shovel (for digging out of snow)
• Chemical hand warmers (available at sporting goods stores)
• Blanket
• Snow chains
• Ice scraper
• Gallon of antifreeze
• Gallon of window-washing fluid
• Cat litter (to provide traction on icy surfaces)

261 How to keep the car tidy

A clutter-free car makes every trip more pleasant. Some strategies:

- Take out what you bring in. Cars can become littered with coffee mugs, magazines, used tissues, jackets, and toys. Train family members—and yourself—to collect their things as they leave the car.
- Keep plastic garbage bags in the car for trash. Keep a stash of recycled plastic garbage bags in the trunk or in a backseat organizer.
- Accessorize the interior. New cars come with built-in accessories like backseat center consoles and storage drawers under the seats. But if you drive an older model, accessorize it yourself. Automotive accessory shops and organization stores sell a wide variety of containers and organizers.

  - Backseat organizers hang over the back of the front seats and can contain kids' stuff—coloring books, crayons, games, and small toys—as well as adult essentials—maps, umbrellas, plastic bags.
  - Front seat caddies can hold coffee mugs, sunglasses, an MP3 player, pens, cell phone, and water bottle.
  - Visor CD holders fit up to twelve CDs (without jewel cases).

- Organize the trunk. (available at home organization and auto supply stores), such as netting, dividers, and collapsible cargo totes (with Velcro bottoms) to secure grocery and shopping bags in place, to hold plants upright, and to contain sports equipment.

262　The Big Move

For an organized house move, keep a:

1. **Master list.** List everything you need to do and the date by which it needs to be done. Writing things down prods your memory, and crossing completed items off the list can give you a sense of progress and accomplishment.

2. **Master file.** Make a file (or files) for all move-related paperwork. Keep contact information, receipts, and contracts from vendors such as movers, storage facilities, charitable organizations (for donations), cleaning services, painters, designers.

3. **Master schedule.** Keep a calendar of your scheduled move date, all vendor appointments, estimates, installations, and any other critical dates leading up to and after the move.

QUICK TIP: **Move Scheduling**

High season for moving is June through September. For better service, try to avoid moving during those months. If you must move during peak season, schedule midweek and midmonth moves (which are less in demand).

263　How to choose your moving method

Consider how far you are going, how much you want to spend, how much heavy lifting you are capable of (and interested in), and how much time you have. Here are the options:

what's a disorganized person to do?

- Do it yourself. Pack up boxes yourself, enlist the help of friends, rent a van, load and unload with your friends (then buy them some pizza).
- Do some yourself. You pack, but movers load and unload.
- Don't lift a finger. Movers do everything for you, including packing.

264 Movers: do your research

No one wants something as important as a move to go badly. Compare rates, discounts, and policies. Check references as well as Better Business Bureau ratings for any record of complaints. If you are moving to another state, check with the U.S. Department of Transportation to ensure that the company is licensed to provide relocation services between states. Have three companies come over to do a walk-through and give estimates. Never accept estimates given over the phone or via the Internet. Two estimates will likely be close together in price and weight; the third will be either very high or very low. Go with one of the two close estimates. Long-distance moves should be based on weight. For short distances, an hourly rate is the norm. (Never accept an estimate based on cubic feet.)

The following are some questions to ask a potential mover:

- How long have you been in operation? (Choose a company in business at least three years.)
- Are you a member of the American Moving & Storage Association (AMSA)?
- Is there a minimum charge for your services?
- Are there extra charges for flights of stairs, obstructed access, or oversize items such as pianos?
- Do you charge extra for evenings or weekends?
- What type of training have the movers received?
- What is your claim ratio (number of damage or loss claims relative to the number of moves)?

265 What to do *before* a move

Toss the junk. Devote a few days (or more if needed) to eliminating things you no longer need. De-cluttering is a critical step in selling a house, since no one likes seeing someone else's mess. Evaluate all your possessions and ask if each item is worth the cost of moving it.

Get boxes. Decide whether to purchase boxes (from your moving company or an office supply store) or procure freebies from a liquor or grocery store. Get the right size box for what it will hold; for example, don't put books in a wardrobe box.

Get other supplies. You'll also need bubble wrap or packing paper (to wrap breakables), scissors or a packing knife, packing tape and a tape gun, a thick marker (for labeling boxes), and a clipboard, pen, and paper (for keeping inventory).

Determine furniture placement. Review the floor plan of your new residence and decide where you will place furniture so you'll be ready to instruct movers about where to put it.

Insure valuables. Check with your homeowner's policy to see if it covers items in transit. If not, insure valuable art, jewelry, and antiques through your moving company.

Transfer school records. Contact schools to transfer necessary educational records.

Schedule a transfer of utilities. Decide what date you will turn off utilities at your old residence and turn them on at your new.

Schedule with gas, electric, water, Internet, cable or satellite TV provider, and phone companies.

Change your address. Contact the post office to forward your mail. You can fill out a form at the post office or do it online at www.usps.com. Mail will forward for up to a year, but be sure to alert friends and family and companies you do business with of your new address as well. Credit card, insurance, and student loan companies usually have a change of address portion on the monthly bill. In addition, contact banks, magazine and newspaper subscriptions, organizations in which you have a membership, as well as:

- Voter registration—check with the local board of elections
- Driver's license and registration—check with the Department of Motor Vehicles in your state
- IRS—call 800-829-1040 or visit www.irs.gov/pub/irs-pdf/ f8822.pdf for change-of-address form (form no. 8822)

266   Packing house

- Pack like with like. Books with books, pots with pots, bedroom items with bedroom items. Do not pack items from different rooms in the same box.
- Label boxes with room *and* contents. Since many boxes will be labeled KITCHEN, noting the contents will help with unpacking.
- Assign a box number to each box and keep a master inventory list. An inventory list helps to ensure that all boxes arrive at your new location and that you know what's missing if they don't.
- Wrap breakables in bubble wrap or paper. Don't overpack boxes that contain fragile items. Keeping boxes light will reduce the chance of them being dropped. Write FRAGILE on a box containing breakables. This way, you can quickly check for damage or breakage at your new home.
- Pack an OPEN ME FIRST box. Consider what items you'll need on the first night in your new place, as well as essentials that will

make moving in and unpacking easier. The box might include linens, towels, tools, lightbulbs, cleaning supplies (including a broom, sponge, and paper towels), toilet paper, toiletries, medications, contact lenses and solution, packing knife (to unpack boxes), and moving-related documents. If possible, take this box with you rather than putting it on the truck. It should be clearly labeled OPEN ME FIRST and be the first box unpacked.

QUICK TIP: **Apartment Moves**

If you are moving to or from an apartment building, be sure to:

1. Provide the building manager(s) with an insurance certificate from your mover. Keep a backup copy for yourself.

2. Reserve the freight elevator.

3. Ask about parking or other restrictions and schedule accordingly.

267 Moving day

What to do when moving . . .

- Count the number of boxes leaving the house. Compare your inventory list with that of the movers and check boxes off your inventory list as they leave.
- Load boxes onto the truck before furniture. Load furniture last so it will come off the truck first. Get furniture unloaded and in place before unloading boxes.
- Do a final check. Walk through your empty home, making sure you haven't forgotten anything. Lock doors and windows. Turn off heat, A/C, and lights.

. . . and arriving

- Instruct movers where contents will go. Walk through your new home with the movers to show them where furniture should be placed and which boxes go to which rooms. Label each room. A sticky note strategically placed on or near the entrance to each room will help movers match box labels to the correct room.
- Count boxes coming in. The number of boxes coming through the door should match the number that left your old place. Check the condition of boxes and open boxes marked FRAGILE to confirm that there was no breakage or damage. Note anything broken or missing on your inventory list.
- Have payment ready. Check ahead of time to find out what form of payment the movers take. Prepare a check or money order or gather cash in advance and have enough cash on hand for a tip.

Resources

Closet Design

California Closets
T 888.336.9707
www.californiaclosets.com

Easy Closets
T 800.910.0129
www.easyclosets.com

Donations/Getting Rid of It

Business clothing for men
Career Gear
120 Broadway, Suite 3660
New York, NY 10271-3602
T 212.577.6190
www.careergear.org

Business clothing for women
Dress for Success
32 East 31st Street, 7th Floor
New York, NY 10016
T 212.532.1922
F 212.684.9563
www.dressforsuccess.org

Junk removal
1-800-GOT-JUNK?
T 800.468.5865
www.1800gotjunk.com

Recycling
Earth 911
1375 N. Scottsdale Rd.
Scottsdale, AZ 85257
T 800-CLEAN-UP
www.earth911.com

Home Improvement Stores

Home Depot
T 800.553.3199
www.homedepot.com

Lowe's
T 800.445.6937
www.lowes.com

Home Organization Stores

Bed Bath & Beyond
T 800.GO.BEYOND
    (800.462.3966)
F 973.785.4255
www.bedbathandbeyond.com

The Container Store
T 800.CONTAIN
    (800.266.8246)
www.containerstore.com

IKEA
T 800.434.IKEA (4532)
www.IKEA.com

Muji
455 Broadway
New York, NY 10013
T 212.334.2002
www.muji.com

Moving and Relocation

Federal Motor Carrier Safety
    Administration
United States Department of
    Transportation
1200 New Jersey Ave SE
Washington, D.C. 20590
T 800.832.5660
www.protectyourmove.gov

Movers
T 866.343.1243
www.movers.com

Self Storage
T 888.342.6673
www.selfstorage.com

Used Cardboard Boxes
T 888.BOXES.88
    (888.269.3788)

Office Supplies

Office Depot
T 800.685.8800
www.officedepot.com

Quill Corporation
P.O. Box 94080
Palatine, IL 60094-4080
T 800.789.1331
F 800.789.8955
www.quill.com

See Jane Work
T 877.400.5263
www.seejanework.com

Staples
T 800.333.3330
www.staples.com

Online Organizing Programs

The Clutter Diet
P.O. Box 40460
Austin, TX 78704
866.915.DIET (3438)
www.clutterdiet.com

The Clutter Prescription
www.clutterprescription.com

Organizing Catalogs

The David Allen Company
T 805.646.8432
www.davidco.com

Improvements Catalog
T 800.634.9484
www.improvementscatalog.
    com

Organize.com
T 800.600.9817
www.organize.com

Organize-It
T 800.210.7712
www.organizeit.com

Organized Living
T 888.674.5484
www.organized-living.com

Space Savers
T 800.849.7210
www.spacesavers.com

Stacks and Stacks
T 800.761.5222
www.stacksandstacks.com

Paper Management

Filing System
Freedom Filer
T 866.553.4537
www.freedomfiler.com

Document Destruction
Shred-it
T 877-60-SHRED
    (877.607.4733)
www.shredit.com

Scanning Software
The Neat Company
3401 Market Street
Suite 100
Philadelphia, PA 19104
T 866.632.8732
www.neatco.com

Photos, Memorabilia, and Archival Preservation

The American Institute for Conservation of Historic & Artistic Works
1156 15th Street NW
Suite 320
Washington, D.C. 20005
T 202.452.9545
F 202.452.9328
www.conservation-us.org

Denver Bookbinding Company
P.O. Box 11187
Denver, CO 80211-3995
T 800.727.4752
F 303.455.2677
www.denverbook.com

Light Impressions
PO Box 2100
Santa Fe Springs, CA 90670
T 800.828.6216
www.lightimpressionsdirect.
    com

Preservation Station
Post Office Box 447
Occoquan, VA 22125-0447
T 571.230.3777
F 509.562.7763
www.preservesmart.com

Professional Organizers

National Association of Professional Organizers (NAPO)
15000 Commerce Parkway
Suite C
Mount Laurel, NJ 08054
T 856.380.6828
F 856.439.0525
www.napo.net

Online Organizing
P.O. Box 655
Jackson, GA 30233
T 877.251.8435
F 206.338.4017
www.onlineorganizing.com

Professional Organizers Web Ring (POWR)
www.organizerswebring.com

Reduce Junk Mail and Unwanted Catalogs

Catalog Choice
www.catalogchoice.org

Do Not Mail
1 Haight Street
San Francisco, CA 94102
T 415.863.4563
www.donotmail.org

Tonic Mailstopper
480 Lytton Avenue, Suite 8
Palo Alto, CA 94301
www.mailstopper.tonic.com

Small Space and Multifunctional Furniture

Lucy Au
4750 Jarry East, Suite 208
Montreal, Quebec H1R 1X8
CANADA
T 514.374.6788
F 514.374.9299
www.lucyau.com

Resource Furniture
969 Third Avenue
New York, NY 10022
T 212.753.2039
F 212.753.9628
www.resourcefurniture.com

Ultimate Bed
T 800.851.9213
www.ultimatebed.com

Storage Solutions

The Art of Storage
125 Washington Street
PO Box 628
Foxborough, MA 02035
T 800.474.6615
F 508.698.3972
www.theartofstorage.com

storeWALL
4119 West Green Tree Road
Milwaukee, WI 53209
T 866.889.2502
www.storewall.com

Stop Telemarketing Calls

USA
National Do Not Call
Registry
T 888.382.1222
(call from the number
you want to register)
www.donotcall.gov

Canada
National Do Not Call List
T 866.580.DNCL (3625)
(call from the number
you want to register)
www.lnnte-dncl.gc.ca

Virtual Assistants

Assist U
T 866.829.6757
www.assistu.com

Elance, Inc.
441 Logue Avenue
Suite 150
Mountain View, CA 94043
T 877.435.2623
F 650.316.7501
www.elance.com

Recommended Reading

Change

One Small Step Can Change Your Life: The Kaizen Way by Robert Maurer, 2004
The First 30 Days by Ariane de Bonvoisin, 2008

Hoarding

Overcoming Compulsive Hoarding: Why You Save and How You Can Stop by Fugen Neziroglu, Jerome Bubrick, Ph.D., and Jose A. Yaryura-Tobias, 2004

Home

Apartment Therapy: The Eight-Step Home Cure by Maxwell Gillingham-Ryan, 2006
Cleaning Plain & Simple by Donna Smallin, 2005
Domino: The Book of Decorating: A Room-by-Room Guide to Creating a Home That Makes You Happy by Deborah Needleman, Sara Ruffin Costello, and Dara Caponigro, 2008

Productivity

Getting Things Done: The Art of Stress-Free Productivity by David Allen, 2001
The 4-Hour Workweek by Timothy Ferriss, 2007
Seven Habits of Highly Effective People by Stephen Covey, 1989

Acknowledgments

My heartfelt thanks to the team at Artisan who put their time and love into making this book what it is: Jan Derevjanik, Nancy Murray, Barbara Peragine, Amy Corley, Chrissa Yee, Erin Sainz, Trent Duffy, and especially Suzanne Lander and Susan Baldaserini, who went beyond the call of duty. Extra-special thanks go to Ann Bramson and my editor, Ingrid Abramovitch, for providing me with the support and guidance in my first literary effort to set down the joys of an organized life in this fun and practical guide.

I am grateful to Susan Spungen for throwing the opening pitch; Shax Riegler, coach extraordinaire and ardent cheerleader; Ben Ritter for bending time—ten-hour photo shoots done in a flash; Elinor McKay, whose time and resources made impossible things possible; Lois Nesbitt for a writer's retreat by the sea; to my clients for providing the perfect laboratories; and to friends and family who supported me through the long process.

For their resources, time, and expertise, I am indebted to: ABC Carpet, Muji, OXO, Andrea Varalli, John Bogosian, Victoria Stein, Nigel Carr, Paul Barnla, Pati Dubroff, Rosina Lardieri, Robin Saidman, Jonathan Pillot, Matt Armendariz, Wayne and Maria Margolies, Diana Siebert Betteridge, Kent Feurring, Kevin and Nancy McKay, Jud Traphagen, Sarah Nina Hayon, Kimberly Flynn, Laurie Sandell, Erica Ackerberg, and Sally S. Lament.

And to my parents, Eileen Olitsky and Stephen Platt, two icons of organization whose genetic material made this book possible.

Index

Photo Credits

Photographs copyright © 2010 by Ben Ritter except for the following:

pages 3, 13, 19, 21 William Abranowicz/
   Art and Commerce Anthology
page 14 ©iStockphoto.com/Mike Manzano
page 20 Goodshoots (RF) /Jupiterimages/
   © Getty Images
pages 22, 66 (top), 67 (left), 103, 121, 134
   (bottom), 157, 161, 184, 195, 197, 222,
   225, 229 courtesy of The Container Store
page 25 Meredith Heuer/Getty Images
page 29 (clockwise from top left) Image
   Source/Getty Images, Monalyn Gracia/
   Corbis, LOOK Photography/Getty Images,
   MIXA/Getty Images
page 36 courtesy of Jokari US, Inc.
   (www.Jokari.com)
page 47 courtesy of H. J. Heinz Company
pages 52, 218 courtesy of Newell
   Rubbermaid Inc. Trademarks
   "Rubbermaid," and the Rubbermaid
   logo, are trademarks of Rubbermaid
page 53 courtesy of Pet Lounge Studios
   (Designer: Corey Drew) and
   www.MyCatsHeaven.com
page 59 (top left) courtesy of Soho Spices/
   Laura Martin
Page 83 © iofoto/Fotolia
page 87 Dan Duchars/Red Cover/Getty
   Images
page 94 Red Cover/Getty Images

page 95 Monalyn Gracia/Corbis
page 104 courtesy of The Great American
   Hanger Company® (www.hangers.com)
page 117 (top left) ©iStockphoto.com/
   Mark Wragg
page 123 ©AVAVA/Fotolia
page 130 Jake Fitzjones/Getty Images
page 139 courtesy of
   www.TheRefinedFeline.com
page 141 Winfried Heinze/Red Cover/
   Getty Images
page 143 Rob Wilkinson/Alamy
page 150 © iStockphoto.com/Christoph Ermel
page 152 courtesy of Skip Hop
page 159 © Paul Maguire/Fotolia
page 163 courtesy of David Allen Company
page 166 © Franny-Anne/Fotolia
page 168 © Digimist523/Fotolia
page 176 © Alex/Fotolia
page 182 © Kati Molin/Fotolia
page 204 © iStockphoto.com/
   Eduardo Jose Bernardino
page 210 © Kirsty Pargeter/Fotolia
page 221 courtesy of The Land of Nod
page 239 Cultura/Corbis
page 253 © Vistas/Fotolia
page 257 (top right) courtesy of Thule/Case
   Logic (www.Thule.com), (bottom left)
   courtesy of Talus Products

TO DO: **JANUARY**	**GOOD IDEA!**	✹ **NEED THIS!**
TO DO: **FEBRUARY**	**GOOD IDEA!**	✹ **NEED THIS!**
TO DO: **MARCH**	**GOOD IDEA!**	✹ **NEED THIS!**
TO DO: **APRIL**	**GOOD IDEA!**	**TO DO** ✓
TO DO: **MAY**	**CHECK THIS WEB SITE OUT** 🖱	**TO DO** ✓
TO DO: **JUNE**	**CHECK THIS WEB SITE OUT** 🖱	**TO DO** ✓
TO DO: **JULY**	**CHECK THIS WEB SITE OUT** 🖱	Share this with:_____
TO DO: **AUGUST**	✹ **I CAN DO THIS!**	Share this with:_____
TO DO: **SEPTEMBER**	✹ **I CAN DO THIS!**	Share this with:_____
TO DO: **OCTOBER**	✹ **I CAN DO THIS!**	**WEEKEND PROJECT**
TO DO: **NOVEMBER**	✹ **I CAN DO THIS!**	**WEEKEND PROJECT**
TO DO: **DECEMBER**	✹ **I CAN DO THIS!**	**WEEKEND PROJECT**

TO DO: **JANUARY**	**GOOD IDEA!**	☀ **NEED THIS!**
TO DO: **FEBRUARY**	**GOOD IDEA!**	☀ **NEED THIS!**
TO DO: **MARCH**	**GOOD IDEA!**	☀ **NEED THIS!**
TO DO: **APRIL**	**GOOD IDEA!**	**TO DO** ✓
TO DO: **MAY**	**CHECK THIS WEB SITE OUT**	**TO DO** ✓
TO DO: **JUNE**	**CHECK THIS WEB SITE OUT**	**TO DO** ✓
TO DO: **JULY**	**CHECK THIS WEB SITE OUT**	Share this with:_____
TO DO: **AUGUST**	☀ **I CAN DO THIS!**	Share this with:_____
TO DO: **SEPTEMBER**	☀ **I CAN DO THIS!**	Share this with:_____
TO DO: **OCTOBER**	☀ **I CAN DO THIS!**	**WEEKEND PROJECT**
TO DO: **NOVEMBER**		**WEEKEND PROJECT**
TO DO: **DECEMBER**	☀ **I CAN DO THIS!**	**WEEKEND PROJECT**